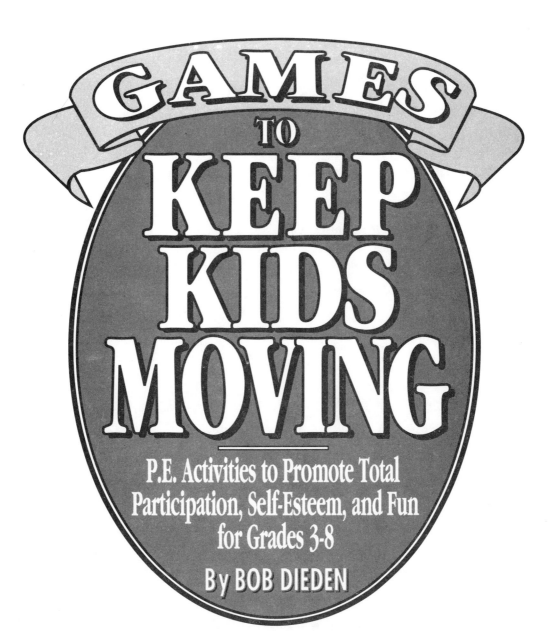

GAMES TO KEEP KIDS MOVING

P.E. Activities to Promote Total
Participation, Self-Esteem, and Fun
for Grades 3-8

By BOB DIEDEN

Illustrations by TOM BECK

PARKER PUBLISHING COMPANY
West Nyack, New York 10994

Library of Congress Cataloging-in-Publication Data

Dieden, Bob.
    Games to keep kids moving! : P.E. activities to promote total
participation, self-esteem, and fun for grades 3-8 / by Bob Dieden ;
illustrations by Tom Beck.
        p.   cm.
    ISBN 0-13-352287-3
    1. Physical education for children.   I. Title.
GV443.D47   1995   95-111
372.86—dc20   CIP

Printed in the United States of America

10   9   8   7   6

ISBN 0-13-352287-3

ATTENTION: CORPORATIONS AND SCHOOLS

Parker Publishing Company books are available at quantity discounts with bulk
purchase for educational, business, or sales promotional use. For information, please
write to: Prentice Hall Career & Personal Development Special Sales, 240 Frisch
Court, Paramus, NJ 07652. Please supply: title of book, ISBN number, quantity, how
the book will be used, date needed.

PARKER PUBLISHING COMPANY
West Nyack, New York 10994

On the World Wide Web at http://www.phdirect.com

PRENTICE-HALL INTERNATIONAL (UK) LIMITED, *LONDON*
PRENTICE-HALL OF AUSTRALIA PTY. LIMITED, *SYDNEY*
PRENTICE-HALL CANADA INC., *TORONTO*
PRENTICE-HALL HISPANOAMERICANA, S.A., *MEXICO*
PRENTICE-HALL OF INDIA PRIVATE LIMITED, *NEW DELHI*
PRENTICE-HALL OF JAPAN, INC., *TOKYO*
PEARSON EDUCATION ASIA PTE. LTD., *SINGAPORE*
EDITORA PRENTICE-HALL DO BRASIL, LTDA., *RIO DE JANEIRO*

DEDICATION

A special "Thank you!" goes to my wife, Corrie, for her understanding, support, encouragement, and gentle prodding when needed. My thanks go also to my daughters, Ria and Rita, who played many of the games contained in this book, and offered their constructive criticism that helped make the games even better.

ABOUT THE AUTHOR

Bod Dieden (B.S., M.S. in education from Northern Illinois University) has designed curriculum and taught physical education classes in Lake Bluff, Illinois, elementary schools since 1960. He is currently athletic director at Lake Bluff Middle School.

Mr Dieden has also coached boys' and girls' basketball, soccer, track, and volleyball. He has initiated an after-school sports program that includes skiing, bowling, roller skating, and racquetball; and he has a long history as sports camp and day camp director, as well as trip director and instructor for a ski club for 28 years.

ABOUT THIS RESOURCE

Two things may happen when students leave a gym class: They may leave disappointed, or they may be enthusiastic. Any number of reasons may contribute to the disappointment. The lead-up games and skill drills may be either too difficult or too boring; the players may not be equally matched when they compete against one another; or students may not be directly involved for most of the game. As a rule, students don't like to spend their gym class standing in line, waiting for their turn.

Games to Keep Kids Moving was designed to avoid these problems and to keep kids eagerly looking forward to their next gym class.

In *Games to Keep Kids Moving*, you will not find games that have winning or losing teams. Players in these games play for self-improvement or team improvement, or to beat time – not other players. Players are constantly moving and having fun, and those who are eliminated are out only long enough to complete a task or get additional equipment.

A very important factor in these games is success, because it helps build students' self-esteem. Many of our softball and kicking games have been modified to allow players – even after they make an out – a chance to go to first base, run the bases, and score a run. In this way, everyone has a chance for success, individually or as a team member. Students in our school have enjoyed playing this way for years.

In *Games to Keep Kids Moving*, you'll find more than 140 games – many with one or more variations. In a few, you will find only two teams playing a game, but most have several teams with three to six players each. The games are organized for 24 players, but you can adjust numbers for your group as needed. These easy-to-understand games were designed to maximize player involvement and movement, and to improve skills. All include *objective, equipment needed, skills, organization of players*, instructions on *how to play, teaching hints* (including safety tips), and *variations*. Most of the games can be played in a gymnasium – with some modifications needed for soccer and softball. Hand-drawn illustrations help clarify team setup, rotation, placement of equipment, and boundaries.

Some of the games being played in gym classes today are the same games many of us played as students, but the modifications in *Games to Keep Kids Moving* make them more interesting, challenging, creative – and especially – more fun. In many of the games, such as "Survival," athletic prowess is not important, but the ability to organize and take charge is. Such games give players with limited athletic ability a chance to excel.

I continue, even after 34 years, to look for new ideas, games, and resource materials that keep kids actively involved with games they enjoy, and – above all – that help them to leave gym class excited about what they've learned and looking forward to the next time. I hope your students will enjoy the activities in *Games to Keep Kids Moving* as much as mine have.

Bob Dieden

WAYS TO CHANGE COMPETITION

Games, for the most part, are competitive by nature. Children enjoy a challenge, and there are ways to have fun while playing competitively. Games can end up in one of three ways: (1) There is one winner – an individual or a team; (2) everyone wins; or (3) everyone works in cooperation to solve a problem. The following are examples of the three ways:

1. An individual or team winner is defined by who won the game. This type of game can also be very competitive, with everyone winning, by just changing the way in which players are rotated. In softball, each team can go through its order during the first inning before switching, with odd-numbered players switching teams to go through the order in the second inning, and even-numbered players challenging the odd-numbered players in the third inning. At the end of three innings, new teams can be chosen.

2. Time an activity and have teams compete against themselves; for example, see how many baskets can be made by the entire group, going to each basket, in five minutes.

3. In volleyball, players can play a competitive game, but in a cooperative way. Count the times both teams can volley the ball over the net, using either a "bump" or "set." With floor hockey, basketball, or flag football, switching sides on the change-over creates competitive games where everyone wins. In all the games we play, we avoid keeping score, and surprisingly enough, the students never ask.

In each game variations section, you will find many other ideas for changing the ways in which games are played. These are just a few examples that have been successful. The final determination of the way your students play the game is up to you.

ACKNOWLEDGEMENTS

I want to thank Donna Parkhurst for her outstanding editing and suggestions; Tom Beck for his clever illustrations which help breathe life into this book; and Ruth Nitsche and Doreen Buksa, with whom I teach, for their valuable suggestions. Finally, I want to thank the students of Central, West, and the Middle School in Lake Bluff, Illinois, from whom I have learned so much.

TABLE OF CONTENTS

SECTION 1
BOY! THESE GAMES ARE FUN — 1

Nineteen exciting and challenging games that make working on skills fun

Name	Grade Level			Play Area		
	3-4	5-6	7-8	Gym	Grass	Playground
Battleball	X	X		X		
Battle of the Quickest	X	X		X		
Battleships	X	X		X		
Blast Away	X	X	X	X		
Bottoms Up	X	X		X		
Escape	X	X		X		
Golden Shoes	X			X	X	
Hoop Lasso	X	X		X	X	X
King or Queen of the Hill	X	X	X	X		X
Magic Wand	X			X		
Mat Ball	X	X	X	X	X	X
Medic	X	X	X	X		
Push Me Home	X	X	X	X		
Run the Gauntlet	X	X	X	X	X	
Scatter	X	X	X	X	X	X
Scavenger	X	X	X	X	X	X
Sharks Are Hungry	X	X		X		
Survival	X	X	X	X	X	
Tired Out	X	X	X	X	X	

SECTION 2
CHALLENGE ACTIVITIES OR CAN I GET THROUGH THIS? — 39

Twenty-three individual or group challenges that bring out the best in everyone

Name	Grade Level			Play Area		
	3-4	5-6	7-8	Gym	Grass	Playground
Bumper Lift	X	X	X	X	X	
Can't Get Enough	X	X		X	X	
Chicken Fights	X	X		X	X	X
Congo Challenge	X	X		X	X	X
Endurance Hop	X	X		X	X	X
Everglades Romp	X	X			X	

SECTION 3
LET'S PLAY TAG TODAY — 73

Ten tag games with a twist that will leave you breathless

SECTION 4
RELAYS, OR, FUN ON THE RUN — 91

Fifteen relays that will bring excitement to your program

Section 5

SCOOTER ACTIVITIES, OR, "POOR PERSON'S ROLLS ROYCE" — 119

Ten Activities that will keep everyone active

Section 6

TEAM GAMES, OR, "SPORTS OF SORTS" — 139

Sixty-eight lead-up games and activities that will challenge even the best athletes

BASKETBALL

SECTION 1

BOY! THESE GAMES ARE FUN

BATTLEBALL

OBJECTIVE: To see how long it takes one team to knock down cone twenty-one times

EQUIPMENT: Four cones and playground balls (7")

SKILLS: Throwing and running

ORGANIZATION: The class is divided into four teams with six players on each team. Two teams will line up along one sideline from half-court to the end line. The other two teams are on the opposite sideline. Place four balls in the center jump circle. One cone is placed on each corner of both free-throw lines. Each player has a number, with the first player on each team lining up next to half-court.

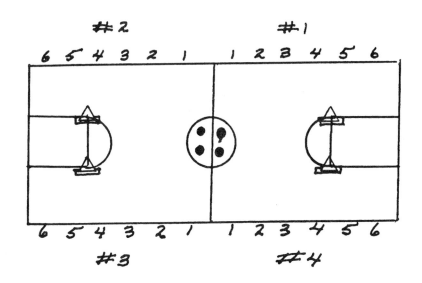

HOW TO PLAY: On a signal, the first two players leave their team. The first player gets the ball. The second player stands next to the cone closest to his or her team. After throwing the ball, the first player immediately goes to the end of the line, whether a cone is knocked down or not. The second player retrieves the ball before running to half-court to throw at the cone. The third player, if the cone was knocked down, has to reset the cone before a player can throw the ball. If a player knocks down a cone by going past the restraining line or receives a ball from a player on the sideline, it does not count. A team does not have to keep the same ball but may use any ball retrieved by the player at the cone. If a cone is knocked down by an opponent, the team receives one point.

BATTLEBALL, *(cont'd.)*

TEACHING HINT: Never throw a ball when another player is between you and your target.

VARIATIONS: The two teams on each half of the gym play against one another—same total score.

Have the four teams attempt to knock down the cones in a set time limit.

See which team, with players going in number order, can be the first to knock down their cone. This team receives one point.

BATTLE OF THE QUICKEST

OBJECTIVE: To receive the lowest point total after a set time limit

EQUIPMENT: Twenty assorted nerf balls

SKILLS: Throwing and dodging

ORGANIZATION: Six teams with four players on each team. Half-court divides two teams standing on each sideline. Two teams also face each other from opposite end lines. The second player for each team will stand either next to half-court if along the sideline or to the team's right if on the end line. The first player from each team will stand at the top of the free-throw circle on that team's half of the gym. Once the games starts, the players in the free-throw circle are free to move anywhere on their half of the gym. All sideline and end line players have a ball to start the game.

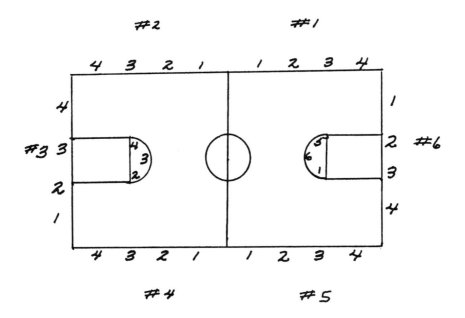

HOW TO PLAY: On a signal, all sideline and end line players roll a ball, attempting to hit one of the players on either side of half-court. Each team must be careful not to hit one of their own. A player hit receives one point and moves to the opposite side of half-court. Players hit twice are replaced by the next one in line. This format is followed throughout the game. Players have to remain behind the sidelines or end lines when rolling the balls, or it doesn't count when a player is hit. A team is penalized one point if a team member hits a player with a thrown ball.

BATTLE OF THE QUICKEST, *(cont'd.)*

TEACHING HINT: Remind the players in the middle that it is safer and harder to be hit if they are not in a group.

VARIATIONS: Have the middle players dribble a basketball. When a player loses control, he or she receives one point and moves to the other half of the gym.

    Players can use soft or foam soccer balls, with players using only their feet in an attempt to hit the middle players.

BATTLESHIPS

OBJECTIVE: To keep the ship from being destroyed

EQUIPMENT: Two scooters, two balls, one tire and one 6′ jump rope for each team

SKILLS: Catching, throwing, and dodging

ORGANIZATION: Six teams with four players on each team. Assign a team to each corner of the gym, with the other two teams facing each other on opposite sidelines (next to a wall) by half-court. Each player has a number from one to four. The tire is placed on top of two scooters and tied with the rope, forming a loop. Each battleship consists of a "captain" a "gunner," and "ammo carriers." The captain (first player) pulls the ship, with the gunner (second player) sitting on top of the tire holding the two balls. The ammo carriers retrieve the balls for the gunner.

HOW TO PLAY: Once the game starts, the captain maneuvers the ship close enough for the gunner to throw or roll the balls in an attempt to destroy a ship. Any ship destroyed has to return to port and replace the players. The captain becomes one of the ammo carriers and the gunner becomes the new captain. Player 3 becomes the new gunner. Any captain hit has to release the rope and help retrieve balls for the gunner. The ship remains in the game but only as long as the gunner can keep the ship from being destroyed. Continue this rotation of players until

BATTLESHIPS, *(cont'd.)*

every player has had a turn to play every position. The ship is completely destroyed when the last player is eliminated. The team then receives one point and starts over. If a gunner catches a thrown ball, the gunner throwing the ball is eliminated.

TEACHING HINT: Remind the captains to use strategy when they chase other ships and to retreat when the ammo carrier is out of ammunition.

VARIATION: Ships on one side of the gym can challenge those on the other side.

BLAST AWAY

OBJECTIVE:	To end up with the fewest points after ten minutes
EQUIPMENT:	Four 16" playground balls and cones, plus twenty-four nerf soft balls
SKILLS:	Throwing, catching, and fielding
ORGANIZATION:	Place four 16" playground balls around the center jump circle. A cone is placed on each sideline by half-court and one under each basket on the end line. Half of each team is on a sideline and half on the end line. Each player is holding a ball.

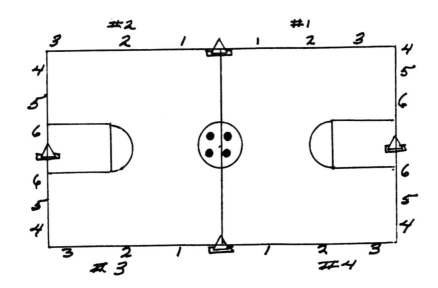

BLAST AWAY, *(cont'd.)*

HOW TO PLAY: On a signal, the teams will throw at any of the balls in the center, attempting to knock it past any of the other teams, as well as preventing a ball from going past the team's own line. Once a ball has passed a team, it remains out of the game. After all the balls have figured in the scoring, the balls are replaced, points are given, and the game is restarted. Players are allowed to move freely along the sideline or end line to protect their own area. Players cannot cross these lines except to retrieve balls that have stopped rolling. If the 16" ball touches anyone or is prevented from crossing either line by a player holding a ball against it, that player's team will receive two points.

TEACHING HINTS: Remind the players to use strategy when throwing the balls, such as rolling a ball in front of the 16" ball to stop it instead of throwing at it. They must never throw a ball when a player is between the one throwing and the target.

VARIATION: Play with six teams. Two teams are on each sideline with the other two teams on the end lines. Place a cone on each corner of a basketball court and one on each side of half-court. Two additional balls are placed in the middle for this game.

BOTTOMS UP

OBJECTIVE: To keep balls in opponents' half of the gym and to end with the lowest point total

EQUIPMENT: One 7" playground ball for every player, and four cones

SKILL: Kicking

ORGANIZATION: Any number of players, divided equally into two teams. Players are in crab-walk position, on their own end line, with a ball directly in front of each player. Place a cone in each corner of a basketball court.

HOW TO PLAY: On a signal, both teams start kicking balls. Players are free to move anywhere on their own half of the gym. After a set time limit (five minutes), play stops and teams receive one point for each ball that goes between the cones on their side. They want to beat this total when they play the next game. The game is started again when teams switch sides and everyone has a ball. Players must have both hands on the floor when they kick a ball. If a player uses hands to hit the ball, penalize the team one point. Return any balls kicked after the whistle to stop play.

TEACHING HINTS: Remind players not to kick a ball when a player is directly in front of them. Turning the opposite hip toward the floor will give them more kicking power.

VARIATIONS: Players use only their hands when in the crab-walk position.
    Have the players stand and use only their hands to strike the ball.

BOTTOMS UP, *(cont'd.)*

Players sit on a scooter; they can use either their hands or their feet to strike the ball. Place two cones on each half of the gym the width of the free-throw lane. Teams receive three points for each ball entering this goal. The lowest point total is the score to beat on the next round.

ESCAPE

OBJECTIVE: For one team to have the most players on its side of the gym

EQUIPMENT: Twelve to fourteen soft or nerf balls for each team

SKILLS: Throwing, catching, and dodging

ORGANIZATION: Two teams with twelve to fourteen players on each team. Players on each team, holding balls, stand on opposite end lines.

HOW TO PLAY: Once the game starts, players may scatter and attempt to hit one another from the waist down with thrown balls. Players of each team may scatter only on their own respective half of the gym. Those hit go to the opponents' end line or either sideline and remain there until they hit an opponent by rolling a ball. If they are successful, players then walk along the sideline until they reach their own side. The player being hit does not go to the opponents' end line or sideline. A player may use a ball to block with, but if the ball being held is dropped, he or she becomes a prisoner. If a player catches a thrown ball, the one throwing has to go to the opponents' end line or sideline. Players become prisoners if they block with the same ball twice in a row.

TEACHING HINT: Do not use fully inflated playground balls or dense foam balls. They could injure a player.

ESCAPE, *(cont'd.)*

VARIATIONS: Players standing behind the opponents' end line may return to their team if they catch a ball thrown to them from a teammate. Sidelines are not used in this game.

Another way to play this game is for those hit to go behind the opponents' end line and remain there even when they have hit one of the opponents. The object of the game is to be the first team to have all opponents behind its end line.

GOLDEN SHOES

OBJECTIVE: To gain the most points

EQUIPMENT: Two tennis balls for each player plus eight specially marked balls. These balls are paired (two for each team) and matched with a master diagram.

SKILL: Running

ORGANIZATION: Four teams with six players on each team. Each team has a number from one to four. This number is on their balls. The game is played in a gymnasium with no boundaries. Each student will place his or her shoes, untied, along with the balls, in the middle of the gym. Players stand on one end line facing the wall.

HOW TO PLAY: The person in charge will scatter the shoes and balls throughout the gym. The specially marked balls are also thrown at this time. On a signal, the players start looking for their shoes. When a player finds one shoe, he or she has to sit at that spot to tie it before looking for the other shoe. Once both sides have found and tied their shoes, the players may start looking for their team balls. When all the balls have been found they may start looking for the specially marked balls. If a player starts looking for the specially marked balls before all team balls have been found, he or she has to start all over, with balls and shoes being thrown throughout the gym. To keep the specially marked balls, the players on a team have to find the team's matching pair. A ball has to be left where it's found until players find the second ball. They may then retrieve the first ball. Each ball is worth one point and the specially marked ones, five points. The highest point total after five minutes is the total to beat in the next game.

TEACHING HINT: Remind the players to watch where they are running.

VARIATIONS: Have the players find and tie their shoes, find their balls, and then line up in a straight line. This is timed; everyone attempts to finish in four minutes. When a player has finished finding his or her balls, that player can either line up or help teammates find team balls.

Play the same game as above, except when they finish the game the players have to crawl through the legs of the players who have already finished.

Have two players, after finding both shoes, tie each other's shoes.

HOOP LASSO

OBJECTIVE: To be the first team to have all the players successfully circle the three cones with a hoop and end up in their original order

EQUIPMENT: Three cones and hoops for each team

SKILL: Throwing

ORGANIZATION: Four teams with six players on each team, each with a number from one to six. Three cones are placed directly in front of each team in a straight line, five, ten, and fifteen feet from one sideline. The first three players on each team will stand by the cones in number order. The fourth player will hold a hoop and stand behind one sideline. Two teams are one each side of half-court or designated area if outside.

HOW TO PLAY: The game starts with the fourth player throwing the hoop, attempting to circle the first cone. The player continues to do this until successful. The player standing next to the cone returns the hoop each time. After the first cone is circled, the player attempts to circle the second and finally the third one. As soon as the first cone has been circled, that player moves to the second cone and the next player in line tries to circle the first cone. This procedure is followed throughout the race. After the first player has circled the three cones, he or she will

HOOP LASSO, *(cont'd.)*

replace the player by the first cone. The second and third players will also replace the players standing by the cones. Any hoop leaning on a cone is considered good. Players may never pass a player in front of them. If a hoop circles an opposing team's cone, the player whose cone is circled may bypass that cone. Only one player on a team may do this. When players are back in their original positions the race is over.

TEACHING HINTS: Remind the players not to throw a hoop when someone is between them and the cone. Make sure players are looking when the hoop is being thrown.

VARIATIONS: Have all the teams work together to finish in a set time. When one team is finished the hoops can be used by any of the teams.

Instead of cones, use hoops and throw bean bags or foam frisbees into the hoops.

Tape circles or squares on the floor and use shuffleboard disks.

KING OR QUEEN OF THE HILL

OBJECTIVE: To be the King or Queen after a set time limit

EQUIPMENT: One 8 1/2" playground ball for each game

SKILL: Striking

ORGANIZATION: Unlimited number, but a minimum of nine players per game. Each player has a number to start the game, and the first nine players will go to the corresponding square, with square 1 being the King or Queen. The queen holds the ball to start the game. Waiting players line up outside the safety area by square 9. Each game is played in an area measuring 30 feet by 30 feet. All balls served are hit with an open palm.

HOW TO PLAY: Play starts with the king or queen hitting the ball with both hands, after the first bounce, to any player in one of the squares. This player, after the ball bounces one time in the square, has to hit it into another square. Play continues until a player makes a mistake. The first player in line then goes to square 9 and the rest of the players rotate up to the square left by the player who made the mistake. A player has to leave a square any time he or she steps on a line, goes out of the square to hit the ball (or after hitting it), returns it to a player who hit it to him or her, fails to hit the ball after bouncing it in his or her square. The king or queen may not serve the ball to the same player or the same square twice in a row.

TEACHING HINT: Remind the players to hit the ball, not palm or throw the ball when they receive it.

VARIATION: Have two players in each square, using the same rules.

MAGIC WAND

OBJECTIVE: To end up with more players remaining in the game after five minutes, or to eliminate one team

EQUIPMENT: Five nerf balls and two plastic golfing tubes for each court (4 courts)

SKILLS: Throwing, catching and dodging

ORGANIZATION: Four teams with six players on each team. Each team is assigned one-quarter of a basketball court. Two players on each team hold the magic wand. The wand is a plastic golfing tube. (You can buy these in quantity at any golf outlet.) A neutral zone is five feet on each side of half-court.

HOW TO PLAY: Once the game starts, players attempt to hit opponents from the waist down in any of the other three courts with a bouncing or rolling ball. Players are not allowed to enter the neutral zone to throw but may retrieve balls. A player is also eliminated when an opposing player catches his or her thrown ball. Those eliminated have to sit on the floor at the spot where they were hit and wait to be rescued by a player tapping them on the shoulder with the magic wand. Those holding the magic wand cannot catch or throw a ball and, if hit, must drop the wand and sit down. Any teammate may pick up the wand and start rescuing the other players. Any wand hit while on the floor is taken out of the game.

MAGIC WAND, *(cont'd.)*

TEACHING HINT: Remind the players holding the magic wand to stay near the rear of their team and leave this area only to rescue someone.

VARIATIONS: A player holding a magic wand, if hit, must join the team that hit her or him.

Allow the person holding the magic wand to enter any team's court to rescue an opposing player. If successful, that player joins his or her team. If the player holding the wand is hit, he or she belongs to that team.

MAT BALL

OBJECTIVE: To score the most runs

EQUIPMENT: Four mats and one 8 1/2" playground ball

SKILLS: Kicking, running, throwing, and catching

ORGANIZATION: Three teams with eight players on each team. Place mats in the far two corners of a basketball court or designated area. The other two mats are placed in line with the restraining line. The mat in the far right corner is first base. The mats, going counterclockwise, are second, third, and home. Two teams, 2 and 3, are on the field, with team 1 starting the game by kicking. Players on each team determine their kicking order. Kicking order determines who pitches each inning. The pitcher stands in the center jump circle when pitching the ball. The second player pitches the second inning. This format is continued throughout the game. The team pitching has to have players covering each mat, with the others playing in the outfield. Team 3 plays only the outfield. There are three outs per inning for each kicking team. After three outs, the kicking team goes to the outfield. Team 3 takes the place of team 2, with team 2 becoming the kicking team.

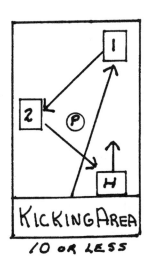

10 OR LESS

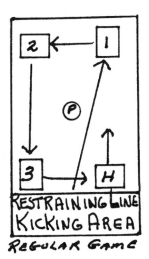

REGULAR GAME

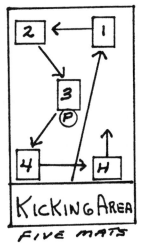

FIVE MATS

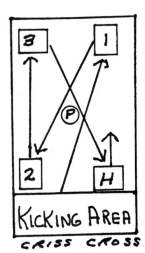

CRISS CROSS

MAT BALL, *(cont'd.)*

HOW TO PLAY: Players are lined up behind the restraining line. The first player, after kicking the ball rolled by the pitcher, runs to the first mat in the far right corner or beyond, depending on where the ball is or how it is being played. Once a runner stops running, the ball is returned to the pitcher. Players kicking the ball make an out by kicking two foul balls (balls that don't pass the restraining line on a fly); kicking a fly ball that is caught, or having the ball hit the ceiling, lights, and beams; or having the fielder covering first catch a thrown ball while on the base and before the kicker gets there. Runners making it safely to a mat make an out only if they overrun a mat or if they reach the next mat after the ball is caught by the fielder covering that mat. If two or more runners are going for the same mat and the fielder catches the ball, both are out, but it is only one team out. If any runner or kicker makes an out, going to the first mat or any other mat, he or she will always return to the first mat and attempt to score again. There may be any number of players on one mat and they may leave in any order. They are not out if they pass another runner. Any fielder standing on the mat and dropping a thrown ball has to throw the ball to another player, who then returns the ball to the fielder, hoping to get the runner. Any fielder catching a throw off the mat has to follow the same procedure. Players do not have to tag up on a fly ball. They should start running on the pitch. If the ball is not kicked, runners are allowed a free walk back to the mats they were on. Any pitcher who fakes a pitch and catches a runner off the mat forces that runner to run to the next mat, and if the ball beats the runner to the mat and is caught, the runner is out.

TEACHING HINT: Encourage the players to be aggressive when running the mats and to advance an extra mat when the ball is thrown away from them.

VARIATIONS: The fielder hits the runner with a thrown ball or catches and bounces the ball on the mat before the runner gets there, to make an out.

Have the players crisscross the mats when running.

Use five mats, with the fifth mat being on the center jump circle.

Play with a whiffle ball and bat, using the same rules.

Play outside and have two games going on at the same time.

Use three mats and smaller teams.

Use four mats and use soccer kicks to advance the ball to a base. Player kicks a stationary ball.

Punt a football to start play, using rules from the original game.

MEDIC

OBJECTIVE: To have more players remaining in the game after a set time limit

EQUIPMENT: Fifteen to twenty nerf or soft balls, four scooters, and four pinnies

SKILLS: Throwing, catching, rolling, and dodging

ORGANIZATION: Two teams with twelve or more on each team. Play the game on a basketball court, with balls being equally divided. Two players from each team are chosen to be the medics and will wear the pinnies. Each team is assigned one half of the gym. Five feet from each end line, and running from sideline to sideline, is an area called "Chicken Gulch." Any player hit in this area has to lie down at half-court. Medics rescue players by placing them on a scooter and pulling them past their own end line.

HOW TO PLAY: Players on both teams eliminate opponents by hitting them from the waist down with a bouncing or rolling ball. Any player going past half-court to throw or retrieve a ball has to fall at that spot. Players being rescued may assist the medic only when getting on the scooter. If a ball is caught on a fly, the player throwing the ball is eliminated. Medics can be eliminated if they are hit with a rolling or bouncing ball, if their scooters are hit, or if a player being rescued interferes with the ball. After ten minutes, or when one team is eliminated, switch sides and medics. A team receives one point each time it has the most players remaining in the game.

MEDIC, *(cont'd.)*

TEACHING HINT: Remind the players that there are times when they have to sacrifice themselves and block balls to protect the medics while they rescue players.

VARIATIONS: Set up mats and use them as forts. If a fort is destroyed, it and all the players behind it are eliminated.

Play by having the medics rescue anyone in the gym. If a medic is hit on the opponents' side, he or she belongs to that team.

Play without medics. When a thrown ball hits an opponent's backboard, all those on that team may re-enter the gam.

Place two pins on opposite sides of the free-throw line. If one or both are knocked down, either by a player or a ball, all players eliminated on that team are allowed back into the game. Play by having each player defend a pin. If the pin is knocked down, that player is eliminated. Players may enter the game if the opponents' backboard is hit.

PUSH ME HOME

OBJECTIVE: To push the tires around the cones in the shortest time

EQUIPMENT: Twelve tires, six mats, and six cones

SKILLS: Running and pushing

ORGANIZATION: Six teams with four players on each team. Place a cone fifteen feet from each corner of the gym and one fifteen feet from each sideline at half-court. Assign a team to each of the cones. Place a mat to the left of each cone and the two tires to the right of the cone. The first two players stand behind the tires facing counterclockwise.

HOW TO PLAY: On a signal, the first two players push their tires to the next cone and give their tires to the next two players in this line. These two players push their tires to the next cone, repeating what the first group did. This is continued until all players have returned to their teams. Those finishing must go to the end of their team line. Any player bumping into anything or anyone must return to where he or she got the tire before continuing. When teams finish pushing the tires, they fold their mats and repeat the same procedure, pushing their mats. Time to see how long it takes every team to get each player back to the original position. Rotate the first two players clockwise and attempt to beat the last time.

PUSH ME HOME, *(cont'd.)*

TEACHING HINT: Remind the first players pushing the mats that they may not leave until teammates have returned with the tires.

VARIATIONS: Roll or carry the tire to the next cone.

Push two scooters first, then the tires, and finally the mats.

Play team against team. Players go completely around all the cones and back to their own team, first pushing the tires and then the mats.

RUN THE GAUNTLET

OBJECTIVE:	To be one of the four runners remaining in the game after ten minutes
EQUIPMENT:	Seven assorted soft or nerf balls for each sideline
SKILLS:	Running, dodging, throwing, and rolling a ball
ORGANIZATION:	Unlimited numbers can play this game. Four are selected, either by birthdays or the date on a coin, and stand in one of the safe areas—ten feet in front of each end line. Boys and girls face one another on opposite sidelines. Those hit in the middle will go to the appropriate sideline. The game is played on a basketball court, or a similar area if outside.

RUN THE GAUNTLET, *(cont'd.)*

HOW TO PLAY: The four players in the middle attempt to run from one end line to the safe area on the opposite side of the gym without being hit, below the waist, with a bouncing or rolled ball. Those hit are replaced by the players hitting them. Only one player may replace a runner at any time. If two players claim they hit the runner, the closest player to where the runner started running enters the game. Any player entering the game must walk along the sideline until he or she reaches the safe area. Any player running directly toward the other players will go to his or her sideline and be replaced by the next player in line. If a player is hit by a player stepping over the sideline, it does not count. Players in the safe area have ten seconds to rest and then must start running. If not, sideline players may throw at them.

TEACHING HINT: Remind the runners that it is easier to hit a group than one individual.

VARIATIONS: Players in the middle have to dribble a basketball when running. A players is replaced any time his or her ball is hit.

When playing outside, have the players dribble a soccer ball. Use the same rules.

SCATTER

OBJECTIVE: To avoid getting hit while attempting to hit other players

EQUIPMENT: Five nerf balls

SKILLS: Running, throwing, catching, and dodging

ORGANIZATION: Unlimited number of players scattered on a basketball court. Five nerf balls are randomly thrown out to start the game. Players have three steps or five seconds to get rid of a ball. Players hit with a ball have to remember who hit them.

HOW TO PLAY: Once the game starts, players hit, from the waist down, must go to either sideline and wait until the player who hit them is hit or they can hit someone with a ball from the sideline. If a player is hit from the sideline, not only the player throwing the ball but all those hit by the same player may re-enter the game. Players go to the sideline if they are hit from the waist down—or if they take more than three steps, hold the ball for five seconds, catch their own thrown balls, or run out of bounds. Any player in the play area may go past the sidelines to retrieve balls.

TEACHING HINTS: Remind the players to watch where they are running, not who is chasing them. Encourage players to be aggressive and go for loose balls.

SCATTER, *(cont'd.)*

VARIATIONS: Play the game on scooters using the same rules.

If ten or more players are on the sideline yell, "Scatter!" This allows everyone on the sideline to enter the game and helps those who took more than three steps or did not see who hit them.

SCAVENGER

OBJECTIVE: To have the most items after a set time limit

EQUIPMENT: Six of each of the following: mats, hoops, erasers, frisbees, whiffle golf balls, roller skating keys, shuttle blocks, deck tennis rings, metal washers, beanbags, hockey caps, hockey pucks, tennis balls, red and white plastic parts of a jump rope, skittle pins, 12" whiffle balls, and any additional items that you may want to add

SKILL: Running

ORGANIZATION: Six teams with four to five players on each team. Place a mat in each corner of the gym and one on each sideline by half-court. If the game is outside, place the mats accordingly. A hoop is placed on each mat with the frisbee inside this hoop. The frisbee and hoop are not taken in this game. Each mat has all of the above items, placed inside the hoop or on the frisbee.

HOW TO PLAY: On a signal, the first player on each team, holding the 12" whiffle ball, runs to an opposite mat, taking one item. The player returns, giving the ball to the next one in line. The item is placed either inside the hoop or on the frisbee, and the player goes to the end of the line. The next player, with the whiffle ball looks for the same item as the one brought back on one of the other mats. This format is continued for a set time limit, such as fifteen minutes. When a team has six of one item, they may take the items off the mat and receive one point. After the time limit, the scores are tallied and items returned to each mat. A list of the items for each mat helps speed up the process when you set up for each game. The score of the team with the most points is the score to beat in the next game. Players may take only one item at a time. If more than one item is taken, the player must return the items, and the team is penalized by

SCAVENGER, *(cont'd.)*

waiting one minute before going again. Two players may not go to the same mat at the same time. A team loses one point if any item is hidden or the 12" whiffle ball is thrown to the next player waiting in line. Players waiting to leave must stand behind the sideline.

TEACHING HINTS: Remind the players to watch where they are running at all times. Allow the teams a few minutes to plan their strategy on which item or items to take. Remind the players that if they see five of one item on a mat they should forget what they were going for and take this item—to block the team from getting a point.

VARIATIONS: Use four mats with the same items—four of each.

Use five mats and hoops, with the fifth mat being placed in the middle of the gym. The middle mat is for any item dropped by a returning runner or when two players are caught going to the same mat. Their items are placed on this mat. Anyone returning may take one of these items. This is the only time two items may be carried.

Use scooters to go to the mats, either individually or with a partner doing the pushing. The one pushing will ride the scooter next, with the next in line doing the pushing.

Have the players dribble a basketball or soccer ball when going and returning.

Give every player and mat a number. After the first game, have the players go to the mat having the same number and start again.

SHARKS ARE HUNGRY

OBJECTIVE: To have all players become sharks

EQUIPMENT: Twelve to sixteen fleece or nerf balls for the marksmen and pinnies for the sharks

SKILLS: Running, dodging, and throwing

ORGANIZATION: Eight teams with three players on each team. Teams number off from one to eight. Team 1 will be the "sharks." Teams 2 through 4 are the "swimmers." The last four teams will be the "marksmen," who are evenly spaced along both end lines and sidelines. Sharks, wearing pinnies, and swimmers are scattered throughout the basketball court.

HOW TO PLAY: Once the game starts, the swimmers attempt to avoid getting tagged by one of the sharks. If tagged, the swimmer goes to the sideline and helps the marksmen. Any shark hit from the waist down with a ball must sit at that spot. Sharks may rescue teammates by pulling them to half-court, then these players may re-enter the game. The game is over when all sharks or swimmers have been eliminated or three minutes have elapsed. Teams on the sidelines and end lines enter the game,

SHARKS ARE HUNGRY, *(cont'd.)*

with one team becoming the sharks. Each time the teams leave the court a new school of sharks is chosen from those entering the court. Players are not allowed to go past either end or sideline when throwing the ball. Marksmen may enter the basketball court to retrieve balls that have stopped rolling.

TEACHING HINT: Remind the players to watch where they are running, not who is chasing them, and not to push when tagging someone.

VARIATIONS: Any shark hit with a thrown ball becomes a swimmer and the player hitting him or her becomes a shark.

Marksmen roll balls at the sharks sitting on scooters.

Same number of teams, but swimmers do not go to the sideline or end line when hit. Sharks receive one point for each player tagged. Sharks are rescued the same way.

SURVIVAL

OBJECTIVE: To be the first team to get all the players and equipment across an open area without the players touching the floor

EQUIPMENT: One mat and two of the following: jump ropes, cones, bases, tires, partially deflated balls, hockey sticks, scooters, chairs, towels, and whatever else you can find, for each team

SKILLS: Throwing, hopping, and working cooperatively

ORGANIZATION: Three teams with eight players on a team. Each team places all its equipment on the mat. The mats are placed behind one end line of a basketball court or designated play area. Each challenge is for fifteen minutes.

HOW TO PLAY: Once the game starts, any player who touches the floor while on a piece of equipment must leave the equipment and return to the end line. This equipment may be taken by a player on any team. Players safely reaching the opposite end line may return (on a piece of equipment) and help teammates. If these players touch the floor they must return to the end line they just left. Any player caught throwing a piece of equipment must return to the original end line. Exception: Tires and scooters may be rolled and jump rope thrown. Any team finishing may assist the other teams. This is a group project and all teams must finish within fifteen minutes.

TEACHING HINT: Remind the players that teamwork is necessary to meet this challenge.

SURVIVAL, *(cont'd.)*

VARIATIONS: If more players are added to one mat this challenge is more difficult.

Take away some of the equipment on each mat to make it even more difficult. Having fewer pieces of equipment forces players to cooperate more in meeting the challenge.

Use only three tires for each team, and no mat.

TIRED OUT

OBJECTIVE: To finish with the most points after a set time limit

EQUIPMENT: Eight tires

SKILLS: Running and crawling

ORGANIZATION: Eight teams with three players on each team. The eight tires, also used as markers, form a large circle. Each team is assigned a tire and will line up inside the circle. The second player in line will hold the tire for the first one in line who is facing the tire. All players will run counterclockwise.

HOW TO PLAY: The first player, after crawling through his or her tire, continues running and crawling through the other tires for one minute. After one minute the second player will run, with the third player holding the tire. This format is continued for the rest of the game. Runners receive one point each time they pass another player. When one player tags another player going through the tire, the one tagging may pass that tire and run to the next one. A player does not have to wait when another player is crawling through a tire. Once a player has gone through a tire, the other players must continue crawling through it unless they tag another player. Any player failing to do this has to return and do it correctly. Any player knocking over a tire immediately stops play. The tire is reset before continuing.

TIRED OUT, *(cont'd.)*

TEACHING HINTS: The players holding the tire must not let it tip forward when players are crawling through it. Remind the players that it is easier to crawl through a tire if they kneel first, then put their arms and heads through the tire.

VARIATIONS: Players run one lap staying to the right of all the tires. On the second lap they crawl through the tires. Same scoring.

Play three on a side. Any player passed in this game returns to the team, with the next player in line starting to run. Once all three players have been eliminated the team receives one point and starts again. The last player left on a team has to continue running until eliminated.

CHALLENGE ACTIVITIES OR CAN I GET THROUGH THIS?

BUMPER LIFT

OBJECTIVE:	For all the players in one group to be the first to complete the challenge
EQUIPMENT:	One 13" playground ball for every four players
SKILLS:	Lifting, pushing, and cooperation
ORGANIZATION:	Unlimited number of players divided into groups of four. The size of a group may also be determined by the number of balls. Pair the groups by body size, weight, and strength. Four players sit in a circle facing the 13" playground ball.

HOW TO PLAY:	The four players in each group place the bottoms of their feet against the 13" playground ball. On command, all the players in the group attempt to lift their buttocks or "bumpers" off the floor and hold for three seconds. If they are successful, have them go again to see how long this position can be held. The body has to be completely off the floor except for the hands. One player in each group will give the command to lift, and will count the seconds.
TEACHING HINT:	Remind the players that it is easier if they bend their knees.
VARIATIONS:	Use a cage ball and see how many players can do this challenge.
	Have the players face a wall and attempt to lift and hold their bumpers for three seconds.
	Have two players place the bottoms of their feet together, attempting the same stunt.

CAN'T GET ENOUGH

OBJECTIVE:	To challenge another player one-to-one
EQUIPMENT:	Depends on the game being played
SKILLS:	Pulling and pushing
ORGANIZATION:	Unlimited number of players divided into pairs. The players in each pair will challenge each other in their own quadrant. All games are played on a grassy surface, or you can use mats when necessary. Players receive one point for each successful challenge.

HOW TO PLAY: Base Challenge. Two players join hands while standing on a base. The object is to make the other player fall off by either pulling or pushing him or her. Challenge another player after five points.

Ball Bump. Players stand on one leg holding a ball. The object is to bump on another until someone loses his or her balance. Challenge is over after one player reaches five points.

Bumper Push. Two players, on all fours, face in opposite directions with feet and buttocks touching. The object is to move the other player past a designated line five feet away. Three points are needed to win this challenge.

Crocodile Challenge. Players face one another in a push-up position. The object is to knock one of the player's arms out from under him or her while balancing on one arm. This is a strenuous activity so play for only one point. Use mats for this challenge.

Grab the Ball. A 10" playground ball is placed on the ground between two players. Both bend at the waist with hands on hips. On a signal, each player attempts to grab the ball before the other player. All players start on the same signal. Challenge another player after five points.

TEACHING HINT: Remind the players that any type of dangerous play is not allowed.

VARIATIONS: Increase the number for each challenge, such as four players holding hands while standing on a mat.

Work with a partner and do the same challenges. The team that has one player left challenges other winning teams.

CHICKEN FIGHTS

OBJECTIVE: To touch another player's knees without having your own knees touched

EQUIPMENT: None

SKILLS: Dodging and eye-hand coordination

ORGANIZATION: Unlimited number of players divided into pairs and facing one another. Assign each pair to an area that has boundaries on all sides. The size of the area isn't important.

HOW TO PLAY: On a signal, both players attempt to touch the other player's knees without having their own touched. When one of the players has been successful five times, he or she will challenge anyone else who is finished. Continue for five minutes. Players may use hands to protect their knees but may not grab or hold a player. The opponent receives credit for one touch when the player he or she is challenging goes out of the area. When two players touch knees at the same time both receive one touch.

TEACHING HINTS: Remind the players to keeps heads up and to use an open palm when touching knees. Encourage them to use trickery to get into position to touch someone's knees.

VARIATIONS: Players wear a flag belt with one flag. This flag is placed behind the player and the challenger tries to pull it.

Play with two flags, with players eliminated when both flags have been pulled by the challenger. Replace flags and challenge someone else.

Use this game as a warm-up for basketball, to teach quick hands.

CONGO CHALLENGE

OBJECTIVE: To be the first team to finish the challenge, keeping all balls in place

EQUIPMENT: One 8 1/2" playground ball for every player: eight cones and two golfing tubes with tabs cut into each end for each team. Use the golfing tubes as shown in the diagram.

SKILL: Cooperation

ORGANIZATION: Divide the players into three teams. A restraining line is ten feet in front of the end line. The first player stands on this line, with the others behind him or her in file formation. The players on each team have a ball pressed against their chests and backs. The first in line has a ball pressed against his or her back and holds a ball. The last player presses his or her ball against the back of the next player in line. Pressure has to be applied to keep balls from falling. Time the activity.

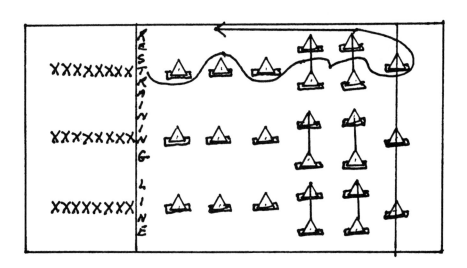

HOW TO PLAY: On a signal, each team has to zig-zag through the cones, go over the hurdles, go around the far cone, and return. Players may not use their hands once the ball has been placed between players. The team must stop and replace any ball that falls to the ground. The team starts over when a player touches the ball with a hand, except to replace it. Exception: Players may reposition their balls when they pass the far cone. Teams do not have to go around or over the obstacles when returning.

TEACHING HINT: Remind the players how important it is to keep a straight line. The best way for a player to do this is to look at the back of the head of the player in front of him or her.

CONGO CHALLENGE, *(cont'd.)*

VARIATIONS: Time the activity and have teams attempt to better their time.

Use this activity as a relay. Have six teams with four on each team. Teams change when they reach the starting line. Balls are repositioned, with each player moving back one position. The last player moves to the front of the line on each switch. When the players return to their original positions, the challenge is over. This is timed.

ENDURANCE HOP

OBJECTIVE: For partners to pick up and return each item – in order, and without touching the floor

EQUIPMENT: Four different objects for each team, such as a beanbag, eraser, whiffle ball, bowling pin, or hockey puck

SKILL: Hopping

ORGANIZATION: Twelve teams, with two players on each team, stand along one sideline. The four items are placed three feet apart and in a straight line. Use tape to mark where the items are to be placed.

HOW TO PLAY: The first player on each team will hop to the first item, pick it up and return, giving it to his or her partner. The first player then returns, without touching the other foot to the floor, and picks up the second item. The second player, after receiving the first item, may leave to return it. This procedure is continued until a player makes a mistake, such as touching any other body part to the floor. Players receive one point for each item picked up and a bonus of five points if they are successful in picking up all four items. A player returning an item may either place it behind the sideline or give it to the partner if he or she is ready. When the first player has successfully picked up the four items, he or she may start again by replacing them. Returned items are worth two points and a bonus of ten points if all items are returned successfully.

TEACHING HINT: Remind the players to take their time and not to change feet.

VARIATIONS: Players have to pick up all the items in one trip. Any item dropped remains on the floor. Players receive one point for each item.

Place a mark every three feet to the opposite sideline. A player, after picking up one item, will place it on the mark past the last item. This is continued until the player makes a mistake, then the second player takes his or her turn.

EVERGLADES ROMP

OBJECTIVE: To successfully cross the swamp without touching the ground

EQUIPMENT: Two jump ropes, tug-of-war ropes, and 18″ cones

SKILLS: Hopping on a cone, grasping, pulling, and carrying own weight over a distance of twenty feet while hanging on a rope

ORGANIZATION: Unlimited numbers of players divided into two teams. Play in an area where the ground is soft and where objects are close enough for the rope to be tied. You can use a tree or jungle gym. Each team has a jump rope, a tug-of-war rope, and a cone. Balance the teams by size, weight, and strength.

HOW TO PLAY: One player from each team, carrying a jump rope, hops on a cone to a designated line. This jump rope is tied to one end of the tug-of-war rope with the other end tied to a tree or another object. Once this player has successfully crossed the swamp by hopping on the cone, the teacher or supervisor secures that end five feet to seven feet above the ground. Any player touching the ground when crossing this area, when hanging and crawling on the rope or hopping on the cone, has to start over. The player hopping on the cone has to wait fifteen seconds before being allowed to retrieve the cone. Once players cross the swamp, a maximum of two players may assist other players having a difficult time. (They may even stand in the swamp to assist teammates.) When every player has successfully crossed the swamp, the challenge is over and time given. This is the time to beat in the next challenge. If both players cross the swamp at the same time, the teams have to wait until both ropes are tied before continuing.

TEACHING HINTS: Have the heaviest or strongest players take the rope across. Secure the rope only five feet off the ground for the lower grades.

VARIATIONS: Use a half-way mark, such as a tree limb or jungle gym, or place bases on the ground, under the rope, where players can rest.

In the lower grades, allow players to touch twice before returning,

Have teams go and return.

Set a time limit, with both teams working together.

FLIGHT TO FREEDOM

OBJECTIVE: To finish the challenge in the shortest time

EQUIPMENT: Eighteen rubber bases, twelve jump ropes, six mats, four portable standards with heavy base, three hoops, three sets of trolleys, and three 16′ jump ropes. Trolleys are made of 4″ × 4″ boards 2′ long. Two holes are drilled completely through and six inches from each end. The small jump ropes are passed through and tied for players to hold while they move.

SKILLS: Running, jumping, lifting, carrying, and group cooperation

ORGANIZATION: Any number of players divided into groups of three. A hoop is hung between two standards and kept in place by tying it with four jump ropes. Four standards are needed for three hoops. Mats are placed under each hoop for safety. The hoops are four feet off the floor. The standards, hoops, and mats are placed in a straight line, starting at one free-throw line. The six rubber bases for each team are spaced 30 inches, 36 inches, and 42 inches apart and staggered. The first rubber base for each team is five feet from the end of the mat. This is the area of quicksand. The last area, from half-court to the far end line, is where the teams use their trolleys.

FLIGHT TO FREEDOM, *(cont'd.)*

HOW TO PLAY: On a signal, the teams, facing their hoops, start helping one another through their hoops. Players, when being assisted through the hoops, may not touch the hoops. If this happens, they start over. After all players have successfully gone through the hoops, they attempt to cross an area of quicksand. Once this has been crossed, they have to navigate the body of water filled with deadly, man-eating gummy bears; two players on trolleys carrying a 16' jump rope held by a teammate waiting his or her turn, attempt to cross this body of water without falling off. If they are successful, the trolleys are tied together with the 16' rope and pulled back by teammates. A player being helped through the hoop may not offer any assistance and must land on his or her feet. Any player touching any part of the hoop will go to the end of the line unless he or she is the last player; if so, the player must start again. Players going over the swamp have to stay on the bases. If they step off, they repeat this part of the challenge only. If either player falls off the trolley, they both return, giving the trolleys to the next in line, and take their places at the end of the line. Players repeat only the part they miss.

TEACHING HINT: Remind the players that cooperation is needed to conquer this challenge and to use extreme caution when they lift a player.

VARIATIONS: Any team finishing may assist the other teams.

Do everything the same way but do it backward.

Use the trolleys by having the partners face each other when they go through the swamp.

Challenge them by having those on the trolleys go over small hurdles and around cones. Players have to work together and lift trolleys to clear hurdles. Do this as a shuttle relay. The players do not go through the hoops. See how long it takes them to go both down and back.

GOING IN CIRCLES

OBJECTIVE: To complete the most laps in five minutes

EQUIPMENT: Eight cones

SKILL: Running

ORGANIZATION: Eight teams with three players on each team. The eight cones, used as markers, form a large circle. Each team will stand between two cones, with the first player on the right.

HOW TO PLAY: On a signal, the first player on each team will step back one pace and run clockwise twice around the circle. When the first runner returns, the second runner will do the same thing, going counterclockwise. After the third runner has his or her turn going clockwise, the directions are changed for the next round. The first and third players go counterclockwise and the second player goes clockwise. Players may pass one another, but they may not touch anyone. Any player going the wrong way has to turn around and do it correctly. Players may run at their own pace.

TEACHING HINTS: Tell the players running clockwise to stay next to the circle and those going counterclockwise to stay on the outside.

VARIATIONS: Players can zig-zag through all the players in the circle.
Players can dribble a basketball while going around the circle.
Players can jump rope when taking their turn.

HURDLE JUMP CHALLENGE

OBJECTIVE: To see how many times a team can jump the hurdles in five minutes

EQUIPMENT: Twenty hurdle inserts and cones (12" or 18") plus eight mats

SKILL: Jumping

ORGANIZATION: Four teams, with six players on each team, line up along one end line. Place two mats, one in front of the other, in front of each team. The five hurdles for each team are placed on these mats and spaced four feet apart in a straight line.

HOW TO PLAY: Players, following one another, jump over each hurdle, using a two-foot take-off. Players continue doing this until a player misses or moves both feet when landing between the hurdles; only a single bound is allowed. The team's score is recorded, and each team goes again, attempting to better this score.

TEACHING HINTS: Remind the players to bend their knees when they land and to use their arms for lift. Have them wait until the player in front has passed the last cone.

VARIATIONS: Use 6" cones and a plastic golfing tube with inserts. These inserts are placed inside the cones. Tubes may be purchased at any golf store. Players jump backward over the hurdle, but their feet are allowed to move. This can be an individual or team challenge.

Have players stand sideways and hop over (Skier's Hop) for thirty seconds.

Have them start the same way but after the fifth jump, landing in a stride position, run ten yards. This is timed.

Space the hurdles two feet apart (6" hurdles). Have players stand sideways, jump over the first hurdle, and return jumping over the hurdle again. The player again jumps over the first hurdle and then the second one, then returns going over the second one, then back over the second hurdle and on to the third one. This is continued until a player reaches the end and it is also timed. Once they have the rhythm, have them return. Good time is twelve seconds.

Use 6" cones and a flexible plastic rod. Players straddle this rod and continue alternating their feet to hop over this hurdle. Once players learn the rhythm, have them start catching a ball while jumping the rod.

JOURNEY INTO DARKNESS

OBJECTIVE: To time each team going through the tunnel and returning

EQUIPMENT: Four mats

SKILL: Crawling

ORGANIZATION: Four teams with six players on each team. Fold each mat into a triangle and place them around the center jump circle. Teams stand behind their tunnels, with the first player kneeling down facing the opening.

HOW TO PLAY: On a signal, the first player on each team attempts to crawl first through his or her own tunnel, past the center jump circle, and through the opposite opponents' tunnel. When the first player has made it through, the next one may leave. Each player who finishes going one way will stand behind the last player in line. Players may not hinder anyone going through the tunnels. If a mat collapses, all the players inside have to get out and reset it before continuing.

TEACHING HINTS: To help eliminate the possibility of injury, make sure players remove their shoes. Remind the players to leave enough room for the other player to get out of the tunnel.

JOURNEY INTO DARKNESS, *(cont'd.)*

VARIATIONS:　　Have the four teams work together. The object of this game is for each player, after going through both tunnels, to rotate one team to his or her right before going again. When players have rotated four times, the challenge is over, with time given.

Have one team and one mat. Have each player go through on all fours and return on his or her back.

Have two tunnels compete against the other two tunnels.

Have the girls challenge the boys.

JUMP TEN CHALLENGE

OBJECTIVE: To see how many beanbags each player can successfully return

EQUIPMENT: Five beanbags and rubber disks for each team. If you do not have enough disks, use 2" floor tape 6" in length

SKILLS: Bending, hopping, and grasping

ORGANIZATION: Eight teams with three players on each team. Teams line up along one sideline. Place the rubber disks every two feet and in a straight line in front of each team. Beanbags are placed on top of these disks.

HOW TO PLAY: The first player on each team, using only one foot, will hop to the first beanbag, pick it up and return to the starting line. The beanbag is given to the next player in line. The player, without touching any other body part to the floor, continues doing this until he or she makes a mistake or picks up all five beanbags. The next player, in either case, will take his or her turn after the beanbags have been replaced. Teams continue to do this for ten minutes. The greatest total of beanbags picked up is the total to beat after the first player on each team has rotated one position to his or her right. After beanbags are replaced, a new game is begun.

TEACHING HINT: Remind the players to stretch for a few minutes before attempting this activity.

VARIATION: Do this as an individual challenge for points. Have fifty or more beanbags scattered around the gym, with a number from one to four on the bottom of each beanbag. Players, while dribbling a basketball, attempt to pick up the beanbags without losing control of the dribble.

KEEP IT GOING

OBJECTIVE:	To see how many consecutive volleys a pair can make before missing
EQUIPMENT:	Two wooden paddles and one tennis ball for each pair
SKILL:	Striking
ORGANIZATION:	The number of pairs is determined by available wall space. Each court is fifteen feet by twenty feet. A line, three feet high, is placed on the wall. Ten feet from the wall is the volleying line. Goggles should be worn or, if they are not available, make sure the partner is out of the way before the ball is hit. One player is holding the ball to start the game.

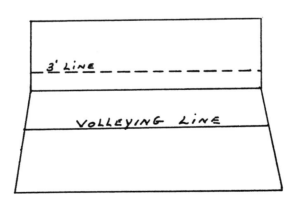

KEEP IT GOING, *(cont'd.)*

HOW TO PLAY: The first player starts the game by dropping the ball and hitting it against the wall with the paddle, then quickly moves away so the partner can volley the ball two times against the wall. These two players, alternating hits, keep adding one volley each time it is their turn. When one player makes a mistake or goes past the volleying line to hit the ball, players start over, attempting to better their score. The ball must remain within each pair's area of safety. Players may not volley the ball more than one time to reach the wall.

TEACHING HINTS: Remind the players to use proper technique when they volley the ball and to call "Hindrance" when they are near another player. For safety, make sure each paddle has a loop at the end of the paddle. All players must insert their hands and turn the loops to tighten them around their wrists. This keeps the paddle from slipping out of a player's hand.

VARIATION: Play with three or four on each team when space is limited.

OUT OF THE RING

OBJECTIVE: To be the only player left on a mat when time expires

EQUIPMENT: Eight mats and different colored pinnies for five teams

SKILLS: Pushing and pulling

ORGANIZATION: Six teams with four players on each team. Four mats are placed in the middle of the court, plus one in each corner. Assign a number from one to four to each corner mat. Players start the game kneeling down on the middle mats. Players receive seven points if they are on a middle mat; five points for mat 1; three points for mat 2; two points for mat 3; and one point for mat 4. Each game will last five minutes.

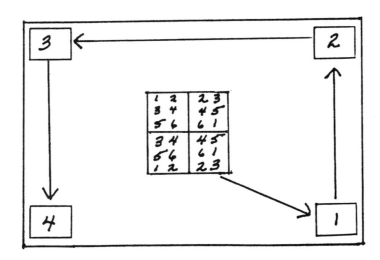

HOW TO PLAY: Anyone pulled or pushed off any middle mat goes to mat 1. Any player forced off this mat goes to mat 2. This procedure is followed until players are forced off mat 4 or time expires. Those eliminated from all the mats jump rope or run laps until time expires. Players who touch any two body parts off the mat, use feet to push players off the mat, or grasp clothing to pull an opponent, have to move to the next mat. Players can team up to eliminate an opponent. The most points earned by any team after four rounds is the new total to beat.

TEACHING HINT: Remind the players to remove all jewelry, eyeglasses, and shoes before playing this game.

VARIATIONS: Play with two teams. One team wears pinnies. Use only the middle mats for this game.
                         Play individually.

POISON PIN

OBJECTIVE:	To receive points by maneuvering a player into the pin
EQUIPMENT:	Six pins
SKILLS:	Pulling, pushing, and quick feet
ORGANIZATION:	Five teams with five players on each team. One player from each team will join hands to form five circles. A pin is placed inside each circle. The five circles are randomly spread out on a basketball court.
HOW TO PLAY:	On a signal, players in each circle attempt to maneuver one another until one knocks down the pin. This player receives one point for his or her team. After five minutes the points are totaled and the lowest point total is the score to beat in the next game. Players can be pulled or pushed into the pin. No violent play is allowed, such as forceful or violent jerking. When two players lose their grip, both receive one point. To avoid this, play can be stopped – if mutually agreed upon – to fix their grips.
TEACHING HINT:	Remind the players that the strongest player doesn't always win; players who use trickery or strategy do much better.
VARIATIONS:	Play individually, with four in each circle. When a player loses, he or she finds a circle with three players in it and play starts again. The lowest point total after ten minutes is the total to beat.
	Play with six in a circle with odd-numbered players going against even-numbered players. Alternate players.

RANGERS AND REBELS

OBJECTIVE:	To see how many Rebels can be forced off the mats in a set time limit
EQUIPMENT:	Six mats and pinnies for one team
SKILLS:	Pushing and cooperation
ORGANIZATION:	There are three teams with eight players on each team. Six mats are placed in the middle of the gym, side by side, forming one large square. One team (Rangers) will wear pinnies and kneel in the middle of the mats. The other two teams will surround the Rangers by kneeling on the outside edges of the mats. Each game lasts for three minutes.
HOW TO PLAY:	The Rebels attempt to force the Rangers off the mats by pushing or pulling them. Any player eliminated, Rebel or Ranger, notifies the person in charge, before re-entering the game. Each player forced off the mat receives one point. Points are added to Rangers' score when a Rebel is pushed off the mat. The Rangers lose one point each time a player on their team is pushed off the mat. After time has expired, the Rangers receive a bonus of three points for each player never forced off the mat. Total the score and the next team will become the Rangers. Each team has two turns to fight the Rebels. A player is eliminated when any two body parts touch outside the mat. Any player using feet to push a player is given a warning the first time, and the team is penalized five points for each additional infraction. Players may not grab clothing to pull someone off the mat or prevent another player from being pulled off the mat.
TEACHING HINT:	Remind the players to remove all jewelry, glasses, and shoes, and never to lift or throw a player off the mat.
VARIATION:	Play boys against boys and girls against girls. Place six mats around the gym and have six teams. One player from each team will start on each mat. Players attempt to push opponents off without getting pushed off themselves. After two minutes, each player remaining on a mat receives one point. Those pushed off the mat remain out of the game. Play again after odd-numbered players rotate one mat to their right.

ROUND TRIP

OBJECTIVE: To see how many lines a player can touch in two minutes

EQUIPMENT: None

SKILL: Running

ORGANIZATION: Unlimited number of players divided into pairs. Each pair is on one sideline. If you do not have enough space, have pairs use the opposite sideline. A line divides the court in half, running from end line to end line. Ten feet in front of each sideline is another line, running from end line to end line.

HOW TO PLAY: On a signal, one partner will count the number of times his or her partner can touch the first line, return touching the sideline, go to the middle touching this line, and return once again touching the sideline. Each touch is with a hand; it does not count if a player just reaches for a line and does not touch it. When time expires, the partner will tell the runner how many lines were touched. The second partner then takes a turn. Each partner has four turns before the activity is over.

TEACHING HINTS: Allow the players enough room so they do not bump into one another. Remind the players to do some light jogging and stretching before attempting this challenge.

VARIATIONS: Have one side of the gym compete against the other side. Total both sides for a future challenge.

    Have four teams, with the team that had the highest number selecting the "Game for the Day."

SIX-CORNER TUG

OBJECTIVE: To be the first player in each group to pick up a pin while remaining within the rope

EQUIPMENT: One tug-of-war rope tied in a knot, six rubber disks and bowling pins

SKILL: Pulling

ORGANIZATION: Six teams with four on each team. Players on each team are matched as closely as possible in size, strength, and weight. The rope, forming a circle, is placed in the middle of the gym or designated play area. One player from each team, placing the rope against his or her waist, will step forward until the rope is taut. Put tape on the floor where each player is standing. Place six rubber disks, equally spaced, six feet in front of each player. A bowling pin is placed on each disk.

HOW TO PLAY: On a signal, each player moves forward, attempting to pick up his or her pin. If successful, and remaining within the rope, he or she receives one point. Six new players will enter the circle while the pin is being replaced. Each player has three turns before the contest is over. A whistle is blown to stop play each time a pin has been successfully picked up. Those inside the rope should continue going for the pin even when they see another player picking one up. Only the whistle stops play. Any

SIX-CORNER TUG, *(cont'd.)*

player picking up the pin and slipping out of the rope has to replace the pin before getting back inside the rope. Give a warning to any player using hands to hold the rope. If it happens a second time, he or she is replaced.

TEACHING HINT: Remind the players to keep their hands in front of their bodies to prevent or break a fall.

VARIATIONS: Have even-numbered players rotate one team to the right and odd-numbered players to the left.

Play with eight in a circle.

Wagonwheel Tug. Four jump ropes are looped in the middle forming eight stations. There are eight teams, with three players on each team. Players stand on a cone and, on a signal, attempt to pull or use trickery to make one of the players lose his or her balance and receive one point. After ten minutes the lowest point total is the score to beat.

TAP AND GO

OBJECTIVE: To gain the most points

EQUIPMENT: Four beanbags and rubber disks, three small cones, and one balloon for each team

SKILLS: Striking and running

ORGANIZATION: Six teams with four players, numbering off from one to four, on each team. The teams use their cones to form a triangle; the distance between corners is fifteen feet. The beanbags are placed on the rubber disks, which are spread out within the triangle. The first player is inside the triangle holding the balloon; three others are at the cones.

HOW TO PLAY: On a signal, the middle player taps the balloon into the air one time, picks up any beanbag and hands it to a player in one of the corners. The middle player quickly returns to tap the balloon once more, and continues to do so, until every player is holding a beanbag. Once this has been accomplished, the middle player reverses the process by taking a beanbag from a player and placing it on the disk. A player's turn is over when the balloon touches the floor or the player has given and taken the beanbags from each player. All four players follow the same procedure. Players may tap the balloon only once before they pick up a beanbag or when taking it from a player.

TAP AND GO, *(cont'd.)*

A turn is over when anyone assists the middle player by tapping the balloon or when the balloon leaves the confines of the triangle. Players receive one point for each beanbag given to a player and two points when returning them to the disks.

TEACHING HINT: Remind each player to hand the beanbag to a player, not throw it, and to tap the balloon in the direction he or she is moving.

VARIATIONS: Use the nondominant hand to strike the balloon.

Make the triangle larger and have the player, after tapping the balloon, pick up and throw the beanbag to a player in each corner.

Play by having the middle players tap the balloon, run around a corner, and returning to tap it again. Continue this until the center player circles all the corners. The next player, without stopping the balloon, continues this format. See how long the players can go before making a mistake.

Place six beanbags inside the triangle. The player taps the balloon, then picks up and slides a beanbag out of the triangle. Continue until all beanbags are out or the player misses.

TOGETHERNESS

OBJECTIVE: To see how many players can remain inside a hoop in a designated time limit

EQUIPMENT: Two climbing ropes, chairs, and hoops, and six mats

SKILLS: Swinging, jumping, and grasping

ORGANIZATION: The number is based on ropes available. No more than twelve to each rope. Swing the climbing rope forward to determine where to place the hoop. Use enough mats to protect students who fall. The first player will stand on a chair held by the next one in line.

HOW TO PLAY: The first player will swing on the rope, attempting to land inside the hoop. If successful, that player will remain there to assist those coming. If the player missed, he or she returns to the end of the line. The other players, taking their turns, continue this procedure for five minutes. After time expires, count the number of players inside the hoop. This is the total to beat the next time. Players touching any body part outside the hoop must get back in line. Players may sit on the knot, hang by

TOGETHERNESS, *(cont'd.)*

their hands, or be assisted by those in the hoop. Any time the chair tips over, the one holding the chair loses a turn and the one swinging goes again.

TEACHING HINT: Remind the players always to face the person swinging the rope and to encourage and assist one another.

VARIATION: Place two hoops, one in front of the other, and attempt to get everyone in these hoops. A player in the first hoop, after assisting someone, has to move forward to the next hoop. Once a player moves forward, he or she may not return to the first hoop to help anyone.

TRY ME — BEAT ME

OBJECTIVE: For players, working together, to complete each challenge

EQUIPMENT: Determined by game played

SKILLS: Depend on game played

ORGANIZATION: Unlimited number of players divided equally into four teams. Challenges can be attempted in a gymnasium or outside.

HOW TO PLAY: Any number of challenges can be created for players to try. Some are:

1. How long can you keep a rainbow ball in the air?

2. Can a group of players get over a 4'-high balance beam, without anyone touching the beam, going under or around the beam, or going over it head first?

3. Can an entire group, holding hands, move a hoop around a circle in a set time limit?

4. Can you move two hoops, on opposite sides of a circle, and have one overtake the other?

5. Can you move a hoop down a straight line and back while all players are holding hands?

6. Can you get an entire team through a hoop held 12 inches, 18 inches, or 36 inches off the floor without the players touching the hoop? (Use several mats for safety.)

7. How many balls can two players carry across a gym?

8. Team Wind-up. Everyone joins hands while standing in a straight line on one end line. The first player on the far right turns to his or her left and continues curling until all players form one tight group. This group has to maneuver around cones, over some tires, and finally over a small hurdle before returning. Any player losing his or her grip forces the group to stop, line up, and wind up before continuing.

9. How many team jumps does it take to get an entire group across an open area? When one player's mark is set the next player will jump from that spot. This is continued until one player crosses the opposite end line.

10. Can an entire team, holding hands, cross an open area touching one body part less than the number going?

11. Can an entire group get across an area 15 feet wide without anyone touching the ground, using only a cone, two ropes and a scooter?

TRY ME — BEAT ME, *(cont'd.)*

12. How long does it take to stack eight tires over a portable standard and then take them off?

TEACHING HINT: Stress the importance of cooperation and teamwork to solve these challenges.

VARIATIONS: Use your imagination to modify or add items to these activities.

TWICE THE FUN

OBJECTIVE: To complete a wheelbarrow challenge within a set time limit

EQUIPMENT: One jump rope for every four players

SKILLS: Lifting, pulling, and pushing

ORGANIZATION: Unlimited number of players divided in groups of four. Place the jump rope on the floor or grass.

HOW TO PLAY: Two players from each team, lying down and facing in opposite directions, place their feet side by side and on top of the rope. The two players who are standing will each grab one end of the rope. On a signal, the players standing will bend down and lift the rope while those on the floor raise themselves into a push-up position. When they move, one player will be going forward with the other one going backward to the designated goal. This is repeated when players return but with roles reversed. Players switch when they reach the starting line and the next two will take their turn. Any player falling while doing the wheelbarrow may not be assisted in getting back up. Players doing the wheelbarrow have to keep both feet on the rope. If a player assists those doing the wheelbarrow the group has to return to the last line touched.

TWICE THE FUN, *(cont'd.)*

TEACHING HINT: Remind the players to take their time when doing this activity.

VARIATION: Have two teams, with four facing forward and four backward. A 16' jump rope is placed under the ankles and held by four players. The group starts at the end line and moves to half-court. When they reach half-court, those moving forward will switch with those holding the rope. When the group returns, those going forward switch and this format is repeated until everyone has gone both forward and backward.

WAGONWHEEL TUG

OBJECTIVE: To have the lowest point total after five minutes

EQUIPMENT: Eight 16′ jump ropes, eight rubber bases, and one tire

SKILL: Pulling

ORGANIZATION: Eight teams with three or more on each team. Tie one end of each jump rope to the tire, wrapping it around a few times. Place the rubber bases ten feet from the tire, forming a circle. The first player on each team will stand on a base holding one end of the jump rope.

HOW TO PLAY: On a signal, the first player on each team attempts to pull another player off base while remaining on his or her own base. Any player stepping off the base or touching any other body part to the ground is replaced by the next one in line. The player being replaced receives one point. Any player releasing the rope to avoid losing his or her balance is given a warning the first time and one point each time it happens again. If two players appear to lose their balance at the same time, give each one a point.

TEACHING HINT: Remind the players that strength doesn't always win but trickery and cunning does.

VARIATIONS: Play individually; if eliminated, the player rotates one team to the right.

Tie ten jump ropes around a tire, having the same number of bases. Play with a partner; when both have been eliminated, the team receives one point. The lowest total wins.

WILDERNESS CHASE

OBJECTIVE:	To see how many laps each sled can make in five minutes
EQUIPMENT:	Three scooters, one mat, one jump rope, and a tire for each team
SKILLS:	Running and pushing
ORGANIZATION:	Four teams with six players on each team, with each player having a number from one to six. Place a tire fifteen feet from each corner of a basketball court. Each team will stand to the inside of its tire marker. Three scooters, one in front of the other, are placed to the outside of the team's marker. A folded mat is placed on top of the three scooters. The first two players, holding the center of a looped rope, will pull the mat, with the third in line pushing. The next three players, in number order, ride on the mat, with the first two each holding one end of a rope.
HOW TO PLAY:	On a signal, all sleds move through the course going counterclockwise and to the right of all the markers. After one lap around the course, each sled is brought to the inside of the team's marker to switch players. The two in front of the sled and the one in back switch with the player or players closest to him or her. This format is continued for five minutes. A team is penalized one lap if it makes the exchange to the outside of the marker or runs into anyone or anything. Each team is given a total and the highest total is the one to beat. Players doing the pulling or pushing move one marker clockwise and those riding on the sled move counterclockwise before the next race. Make this switch every five minutes.
TEACHING HINT:	Remind the players that control is more important than speed.
VARIATIONS:	Run the same course, but have each sled go around twice before switching.

Play the same game, but place an extra tire on each free-throw line and another one fifteen feet from the center jump circle. Teams have to go to the left or inside these markers. |

SECTION 3

LET'S PLAY TAG TODAY

BALLOON TAG

OBJECTIVE: To avoid becoming "It"

EQUIPMENT: Four to five balloons

SKILLS: Running, dodging, and striking

ORGANIZATION: Unlimited number of players spread out on a basketball court. Four or five players are selected to be "It" and hold a balloon. Those with the balloon may take as many steps as necessary when they chase players.

HOW TO PLAY: Each player who is "It" strikes the balloon, attempting to hit the other players and if successful, will change places with the player hit. Players must remain within the boundaries of a basketball court. Anyone running out of bounds to avoid getting caught will change places with the player chasing him or her. Any player hit with the balloon can avoid becoming "It" if he or she can catch the balloon before it touches the floor. If successful, this player can tap the balloon away from "It."

BALLOON TAG, *(cont'd.)*

TEACHING HINT: Remind the players to watch where they are running, not who is chasing them.

VARIATIONS: Play the same way, but those who are "It" do not change places when hitting someone. They continue chasing for four minutes. Those hit will sit at that spot and remain there until a player catches a balloon. This allows everyone sitting to re-enter the game.

Assign teams and have each team play for three or four minutes. Those who are "It" receive one point each time they hit a player. Players who are hit do not leave the game. The highest point total is the new total to beat.

BOG TAG

OBJECTIVE: For those who are "It" to tag as many players as possible to receive points

EQUIPMENT: Ten rubber bases and two pinnies

SKILLS: Running and dodging

ORGANIZATION: Unlimited number divided into pairs, with each pair given a number. The rubber bases are scattered on the basketball court or play area; each base is given a number from one to ten. The first pair will start the game as "It" and, in writing, will determine which five bases will be quicksand, or "bogs." Those who are "It" will wear the pinnies.

HOW TO PLAY: Those who are "It" attempt to tag as many players as possible or force them to run out of bounds; any player caught has to sit at that spot. Those not caught may rescue these players by sitting back-to-back, hooking elbows, and trying to stand – keeping elbows hooked. If they are successful, the rescued player may re-enter the game. After three minutes, those who are "It" will yell, "Bogs!" Those not sitting quickly run to any of the ten bases. "It" will inform those who are standing on the bogs. They, and those who are caught, are worth one point each. Points are totaled and the next group will become "It." Continue this format until every pair has had a turn.

BOG TAG, *(cont'd.)*

TEACHING HINTS: Remind the players to watch where they are running and not to look at who is chasing them. Have those who are "It" select new bases as bogs for each game.

VARIATION: Players use basketballs and have to keep control of their balls while being chased. If they do not, and they commit a dribbling violation, they go to one of the baskets and must make five lay-ups before re-entering the game. Points are totaled the same way.

CONTINUOUS SQUARE TAG

OBJECTIVE: To see how long a player can remain in Area One

EQUIPMENT: None

SKILLS: Running and dodging

ORGANIZATION: Unlimited number of players in a scattered formation. Three areas are set up, with Area One being the largest and outside the boundaries of a basketball court. Area Two is inside the boundaries and is smaller than Area One. Area Three, the smallest area, is inside a volleyball court. Everyone starts the game in Area One.

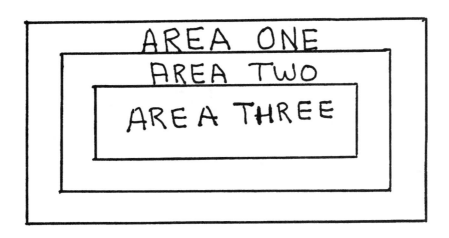

HOW TO PLAY: On a signal, players attempt to tag another player's knees before being tagged themselves. Any player tagged will go to Area Two. If tagged again, this player will enter Area Three. Any time players tag someone, they may enter the next largest area, if they are not already in Area One. Any player leaving any area to avoid getting tagged must enter the next lowest area. If two players touch each other's knees at the same time, both move to the next lowest area. Players are allowed to use hands to protect their knees. Each game lasts for two minutes.

TEACHING HINT: Remind the players to watch where they are running, not who is chasing them.

VARIATION: Set up teams and play the same way. After two minutes count how many from each team remain in each area. The points given are the same as the area number. The lowest point total, after playing two rounds, is the score to beat.

CROCODILE TAG

OBJECTIVE: To avoid becoming "It"

EQUIPMENT: None

SKILLS: Running and dodging

ORGANIZATION: Select two players to be "It." The remaining players, spreading out, have to remain within the boundaries of a basketball court or other designated area.

HOW TO PLAY: Once the game starts, players being chased are safe when they assume a crocodile (isometric push-up) position for the count of three. If those who are "It" guard a player longer than three seconds, the player is allowed a free run. Players intentionally getting caught should be warned. If it happens a second time, have the player pay a penalty (sit two minutes) before re-entering the game. Any player caught automatically becomes the new "It."

TEACHING HINT: Remind the players never to jump over a player in the crocodile position or push when they tag someone.

VARIATIONS: Issue pinnies and have four to five players be "It." When players are tagged they have to get into an isometric push-up position. These players can be rescued when another player assumes the same position and they both slap right hands.

CROCODILE TAG, *(cont'd.)*

Ventriloquist Tag. In this game players are safe when sitting on another player's knee.

Pony Express Tag. Player is safe when on someone's back. Have the players dribble a basketball, and when tagged, change places with "It" and give that person the ball. Those who are "It" do not have balls.

HELP

OBJECTIVE: To avoid getting tagged and to help those being chased

EQUIPMENT: One 7" nerf ball for every third player, plus three pinnies

SKILLS: Running, dodging, throwing, and catching

ORGANIZATION: Unlimited number of players in a scattered formation on a basketball court. Three players are "It" and wear pinnies and hold balls.

HOW TO PLAY: Those who are "It" attempt to tag any player without a ball. Those tagged go to either sideline to run two laps before re-entering the game. Any player being chased can be saved if a ball is thrown to him or her before being tagged. The one chasing has to leave immediately and start chasing someone else. Players are caught if they run out of bounds, are tagged without a ball, drop a thrown ball, or hold the ball for more than five seconds.

TEACHING HINTS: Remind the players to watch where they are running and not to look at who is chasing them. Tell the players it is easier to catch a ball when they know it is coming; they should call out a player's name before throwing the ball.

VARIATION: Use the same rules, but have the players dribble a soccer or basketball, which is passed to those in trouble.

I NEED ROOM

OBJECTIVE: For those who are "It" to pull flags, earning points

EQUIPMENT: One set of flags for every player, four mats, three pinnies, and one flag box with extra flags

SKILLS: Running and dodging

ORGANIZATION: Unlimited number of players divided into groups of three. Each group is assigned a number based on the number playing. A mat is placed in each corner of a basketball court. These mats are safe areas for a maximum of five players. Group 1 starts the game being "It," with the other players spreading out on the basketball court. The time each group is "It" is determined by the number of groups playing the game and the time available.

FLAG
BOX

I NEED ROOM, *(cont'd.)*

HOW TO PLAY: "It" chases the other players; when players lose both flags they go to the flag box to get two more. "It" may take only one flag from a player. Five players are safe on a mat but when another player arrives, all five must leave. A player is considered caught and will lose one flag if he or she goes past court boundaries and when both flags have been pulled.

TEACHING HINT: Remind the players to keep running, not to stop and stand on the mats.

VARIATION: Play the same game but add a mat to each sideline by half-court. Allow one player on a mat at any one time. Have five or six be "It."

ISLAND HOPPING

OBJECTIVE: To avoid getting caught and to be lucky enough not to run to one of the "sinking islands"

EQUIPMENT: Five mats and two pinnies

SKILLS: Running, dodging, and pulling

ORGANIZATION: Unlimited number of players in a scattered formation on a basketball court. Number five mats and space them a minimum of twenty-five feet apart to form one very large circle. Two players are selected to be "It." They wear pinnies and select two of the islands to be the sinking islands, writing down their numbers.

HOW TO PLAY: "It" starts chasing the other players and anyone caught has to sit at that spot. These players may be rescued when a player pulls them to any of the mats. A player reaching one of the mats forces any other player off the mat; only one player at a time may be on a mat. After three minutes, "It" calls out, "Islands!" Those not sitting down run to one of the five mats. Those on the mats are told which mats are the sinking islands. Players on the sinking islands, and those caught but not rescued receive one point each. Two new players are chosen from those not caught. Any player running out of bounds or jumping over other players will sit at that spot. When two players run to the same mat, both have to leave and find another mat.

ISLAND HOPPING, *(cont'd.)*

TEACHING HINT: Remind the rescuers and the players being rescued that they must grab one another's wrists and be careful not to drop the player being rescued.

VARIATIONS: Play with six teams. Teams receive one point for each player caught.

Keep the same teams, but everyone wears flags. Any flag pulled is worth one point. If a player loses both flags he or she may go to the flag box and get extra flags.

KICK AND CHASE

OBJECTIVE: To receive points by tagging players

EQUIPMENT: Six pinnies, one 7" playground ball, and one hoop

SKILLS: Kicking, running, dodging, catching, and throwing

ORGANIZATION: Four teams, with six players on each team, number off from one to four. Place a hoop in the middle of a large circle measuring fifteen feet in diameter. Team 1, wearing pinnies, and standing around this circle, will start chasing players after a player on this team kicks the ball.

HOW TO PLAY: Team 1 will continue to chase and tag as many players as possible before the ball is returned to the hoop by any player from the three other teams. Each game lasts four minutes and players being chased can be tagged by more than one chaser. When the ball is placed in the hoop, the game stops and the team doing the chasing receives one point for each player tagged. Continue this format with the three other teams. The player retrieving the ball may take a maximum of five steps when holding the ball but unlimited steps when dribbling it. Any player taking more than five steps when holding the ball, or dropping a thrown ball, picks it up and has to give the ball to the team doing the chasing. That team is given a free kick, with play starting again.

TEACHING HINTS: Remind the players to use strategy to get the ball to the hoop. The team doing the chasing should assign one player to guard the hoop.

VARIATIONS: Use a football and use same rules.

Inside, use a basketball and, play with six on a team. One team is "It," and one team in pinnies, is shooting baskets. The last two teams are chased by those who are "It." Each player on the shooting team has to make one basket before play stops. They are not chased and may retrieve the ball for the player shooting. Players in this game, when tagged, must be rescued by being pulled to the nearest end line before reentering the game. If all the players are caught before the team is finished shooting, the team who is "It" receives five bonus points for each player not finishing his or her turn.

PARTNER TAG

OBJECTIVE: For partners to tag other players without being tagged

EQUIPMENT: None

SKILLS: Running and dodging

ORGANIZATION: Unlimited number of players divided into pairs. The game is played on a basketball court or similar area, with players spread out. Partners hold hands; one pair is "It."

HOW TO PLAY: Once the game starts, any player tagged or any player running out of bounds has to sit at that spot. The player without a partner has ten seconds to find a new partner from those who also lost a partner. If the player is not successful within ten seconds, he or she also has to sit. Tagged players may re-enter the game if they can tag anyone running by them. The ten-second rule also applies in this case. When two players tag each other at the same time, both have to sit. Start a new game every five minutes.

TEACHING HINTS: Remind the players never to jump over anyone sitting. Partners must make sure they are running in the same direction.

VARIATION: One partner dribbles while the other one attempts to knock balls away from the other pairs. If the attempt is successful, the player losing control switches positions with his or her partner. If this player loses control of the dribble, the pair receives one point and they go again. The lowest point total after ten minutes is the new total to beat.

UP FOR GRABS

OBJECTIVE: To avoid getting tagged

EQUIPMENT: Two complete flag sets

SKILLS: Running and dodging

ORGANIZATION: Unlimited number scattered on a basketball court or designated area. Two players are chosen to be "It" and wear the flags.

HOW TO PLAY: Once the game starts, any player getting tagged or running out of bounds will stand on one sideline and wait to be rescued. Players are rescued when any player pulls a flag from those who are "It." Any flag lost by "It" remains out of the game. When a player pulls the last flag from "It" he or she becomes the new "It." Every three or four minutes, pick two new players to be "It" from those still in the game.

TEACHING HINT: Remind the players that one player working alone makes it very difficult to pull a flag. Working together and using strategy works much better.

VARIATION: Play in teams. See how long it takes for those who are "It" to lose their flags. This is the time to beat.

SECTION 4

RELAYS,
OR,
FUN ON THE RUN

BLUFF 500

OBJECTIVE: To be the first team to finish the race. This is timed.

EQUIPMENT: Twelve scooters, six tires, six cones, and six 16' jump ropes

SKILLS: Running and pulling

ORGANIZATION: The cones are used to form one large circle on a basketball court. There are six teams with four players on each team. Each team is assigned a cone and will line up to the inside of this cone. Players number off from one to four. The chariot (two scooters with a tire on top) is placed to the right of the cone facing counterclockwise. The jump rope is tied together around the tire and held by the first and second player in line. The two sitting on the chariot also hold the rope. The winning team sets the time to beat in the next race.

HOW TO PLAY: On a signal, the chariots are pulled two times around the course, staying to the right of all the cones. When the two rounds are finished, the chariot is pulled to the left of the cone for the exchange. The first player will change places with the third player. The second and third players now pull, with the fourth and first riding the chariot. Follow this procedure until every player has pulled twice. A chariot running into anything or anyone is given a warning the first time. If it happens again with the same two players, the team is penalized by having those two do one more lap. If an exchange is made to the right of the cone, a team is penalized ten seconds. The chariot is moved to the proper area and remains there for an additional ten seconds. Any time the chariot falls apart, only the two riding on it may fix it.

BLUFF 500, *(cont'd.)*

TEACHING HINT:	Remind the players to shorten up on the rope when turning the corners and to slow down when approaching another chariot.
VARIATION:	Run this race as a relay to see who finishes first.

FIGURE EIGHT RELAY

OBJECTIVE: To see how long it takes each team to run the circuit

EQUIPMENT: Four white bases and four orange bases

SKILL: Running

ORGANIZATION: Eight teams with three players on each team. Bases are arranged in a figure eight design and approximately forty feet apart. The white bases are the even-numbered bases. A team is assigned to each base. The first runner on each team will stand on the base, with teammates one step away.

HOW TO PLAY: On a signal, the first one in line will run the bases in number order, based on where he or she is starting. The next runner may leave when the one in front has passed the team's base. Any player missing a base has to return and touch the base before continuing. Any player, passing another runner, may bypass the next base, but must continue running the same pattern. A team is finished when every player has completed five turns. The time of the first team finished is the time to beat in the next race.

TEACHING HINT: Remind the players to pass other players on their right and to run on the balls of their feet.

VARIATIONS: Players run the race the same way but when they finish they go to the end of the next team's line. The object is to see how long it takes everyone to return to the original place in line.

FIGURE EIGHT RELAY, *(cont'd.)*

Dribble a soccer or basketball around the bases. Go to the next team and give the ball to the next player waiting before going to the end of that line. Players continue doing this until they are back to their original position. This is also timed.

GASP, GASP RELAY

OBJECTIVE: To be the team making the most trips in five minutes

EQUIPMENT: Ten cones and a basketball for every player

SKILLS: Dribbling and running

ORGANIZATION: Six teams with four players on each team. Place the cones according to the diagram. One team will stand in each corner of the gym behind the sideline and in file formation. The remaining two teams line up on opposite sidelines by half-court. The first player on each team is holding a basketball. The teams number off from one to six.

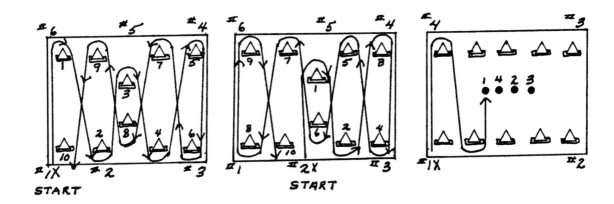

HOW TO PLAY: On a signal, the first player on each team will start dribbling the ball around all the cones, taking them in order from the starting place. The next player, may leave when the player in front of him or her has passed the third cone. Any player committing a dribbling violation or going the wrong way past a cone has to return and do it correctly.

TEACHING HINT: Remind the players to dribble under control and that the first player reaching a cone has the right-of-way.

VARIATIONS: Run the course the same way. When players finish, they rotate one team to the right and continue to do so until they return to their original positions. This is timed.

Four teams – each team in a corner. Four pins are placed and numbered in the middle of the gym. The object is to be the first player, while running the course, to pick up the team's pin. The team receives one point and the pins are replaced.

GO AND GET 'EM

OBJECTIVE: To pass players without being passed

EQUIPMENT: Twelve 18″ cones and six hurdle inserts. Grade 3 uses 12″ cones.

SKILLS: Running and jumping

ORGANIZATION: Six teams with four on each team. Two cones on each half of a basketball court are placed midway between each sideline and the free-throw line. One cone is placed five feet from each end line and in the middle of the free-throw lane. The hurdles are placed according to the diagram. The first player on each team will stand to the right of his or her cone, facing counter-clockwise. Teammates are to the inside and facing the cone. The teams count off, with each team being assigned a cone.

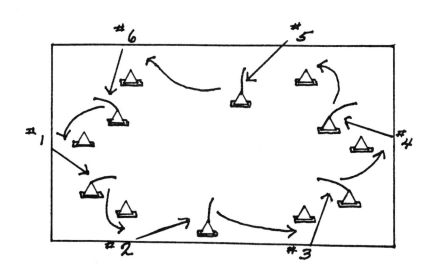

GO AND GET 'EM, *(cont'd.)*

HOW TO PLAY: On a signal, the first player on each team will jump over all the hurdles, staying to the right of all cones, before returning. The next players follow the same procedure. Each player passed receives one point. Anyone knocking over a hurdle has to replace it before continuing. Anyone running on the wrong side of a cone must return and do it correctly. Any hurdle being replaced may be by-passed by the other runners until it is set up.

TEACHING HINTS: Tell the players to use strategy by waiting a split second before starting. In this way, the runner ends up chasing someone instead of being chased. For safety, players may not touch other players.

VARIATIONS: Have each player finishing rotate one team to the right, if he or she was not passed during his or her turn. The object is to see how long it takes each team to return to its original position.

Use a scooter to run the course, but stay to the right of all cones while going under the hurdles.

Have each player continue running until she or he is passed by another player or a certain time limit is reached, such as one minute. Players left in the game receive one point. The highest point total after each player has four turns is the score to beat next time.

HOOP CROQUET

OBJECTIVE: For players, in number order, to run as many circuits as possible in ten minutes

EQUIPMENT: Ten hoops and holders plus two cones for each field

SKILLS: Running and crawling

ORGANIZATION: Four teams with six players on each team. Set up according to the diagram. Players number off from one to six; teams number off from one to four. Two teams challenge each other on each field. There is a buffer zone five feet wide between the two fields. Players line up in a straight line behind their starting line, facing the first hoop.

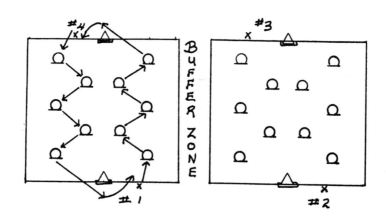

HOOP CROQUET, *(cont'd.)*

HOW TO PLAY: The first player on each team will run and crawl through the five hoops directly in front of him or her, go around the cone, and repeat the course when returning. When the first player has passed the far cone, the next player in line may leave. This procedure is followed for ten minutes. Any player leaving before the far cone is passed has to return and do it correctly before continuing. Each player finishing will return to the end of the line. Players may by-pass a hoop if they pass or tag a runner approaching or going through a hoop. Any hoop knocked down has to be replaced by that player. If a hoop is not replaced before the next runner arrives, this runner may also by-pass that hoop.

TEACHING HINTS: Make sure the area is safe from any hazards when playing outside. Remind the players to pass another runner on the right and not to tag anyone, unless that player is tagged going through a hoop.

VARIATIONS: Dribble a basketball (inside) or a soccer ball (outside) to the left of the first, third, and fifth hoop and to the right of the other two.

Have the player, when finishing, go to the opponents' team on the next field. Time to see how long it takes to get everyone back to the original team position.

Play "Cut-throat." Players attempt to tag the player in front of them without being tagged themselves. If the player is tagged, the next player in line leaves immediately. The player tagged receives one point and returns, taking his or her place in line. Play for fifteen minutes. The lowest point total is the new total to beat in the next game.

HOT AIR VOLLEY

OBJECTIVE: To keep a balloon from touching the floor

EQUIPMENT: Five balloons and five wands

SKILL: Striking

ORGANIZATION: Five teams with five players on each team and each having a number from one to five. The first and third players hold a wand, with the second and fourth players facing each other on opposite sides of the wand. The fifth player stands behind player 4. Each team will line up along the sideline. Players' movement is counterclockwise. The fourth player holds the balloon. The wand is always held shoulder height.

HOW TO PLAY: The game starts with the fourth player hitting the balloon over the wand to the second player and moving to take player 1's position. Player 1 waits until player 2 has returned the balloon to player 5 before taking the place of player 2. Player 2, after hitting the balloon back over the wand, will take the place of player 3 who then stands behind player 5. Players continue to rotate one position to their right each time the balloon is hit over the wand. Players may hit the balloon as many times as needed to get it over the wand. Players holding the wand may move sideways but may not catch the balloon or lower the wand to assist teammates. Two players must be holding the wand before the balloon can be hit over it. If a wand is dropped while the players are changing places and the balloon has been hit, the wand has to be picked up quickly before the balloon goes over it, or a team receives one point. The lowest point total after five minutes is the new total to beat.

HOT AIR VOLLEY, *(cont'd.)*

TEACHING HINTS: Remind the players that proper rotation and hitting the balloon as high as possible will help guarantee success. Encourage teams to remain within their own lane at all times.

VARIATION: Set teams in groups of four. In this game, two players hold the wand while the other two hit the balloon back and forth until all four reach the opposite sideline. Players switch without stopping play and return. The object is to see how many trips a team can make.

HUMAN OBSTACLE COURSE

OBJECTIVE: To see how many times each team can run the course in ten minutes

EQUIPMENT: Twelve rubber disks and six cones

SKILLS: Running, leaping, and crawling

ORGANIZATION: Six teams, with four players on each team, line up along one sideline. Place a disk thirty feet and forty-five feet from one sideline for each team. The cones are placed on the opposite sideline. Players number off from one to four, with the first player kneeling on all fours on the first mark. The second player is standing with feet shoulder width apart on the second mark. The remaining two players are behind the sideline.

HOW TO PLAY: On a signal, the first player in line will leapfrog over the first player, crawl through the legs of the second player, run around the cone, and return, with the next player leaving when the beginning sideline is passed. Players rotate in number order. The player finishing will replace the kneeling player. This player would then replace the player who is standing. On the next rotation, players follow the same format, with the last player going to the end of the line. Any player leaving before the teammate has passed the sideline has to return and start over. Players must place their hands on the shoulders of the players they are leaping over. The total number of trips in ten minutes is the new total for all teams to beat.

TEACHING HINT: Remind the players being jumped over to keep their heads down and to brace themselves so as not to fall forward.

VARIATIONS: Run the course the same way, but have the players run around the far cone, then crawl through and leapfrog over the two players on the field.

HUMAN OBSTACLE COURSE, *(cont'd.)*

Run the race with the players on each team circling the two players and the cone before returning.

Push a scooter around the far cone and return, going between the legs of the two players. Those on the scooter have to be lying down to do this.

I LOST MY PADDLE

OBJECTIVE: To complete the assigned task without the players' changing positions

EQUIPMENT: Three scooters, two cones, and one mat for each team

SKILLS: Pushing and pulling

ORGANIZATION: Six teams with four players on each team. All six teams, spaced a minimum of fifteen feet apart, line up along one sideline. One cone is placed next to each team, with the other cone placed on the opposite sideline directly in front of each team. A folded mat is placed on top of the three scooters.

HOW TO PLAY: The four players from each team lie on their mat, with two facing forward and two facing the rear. The players pull and push the mat around the far cone and return, going around the cone on the starting line. Once past this cone, the players reverse the mat. Those who pulled will now push and those who pushed will pull. Each player may use only one hand to pull or push the mat. Penalize a team if any player is caught using two hands. The mat must turn in two full circles before continuing. When a team finishes six trips, the race is over and time is given. The two players facing forward in the first game will rotate one team to the right and face the rear; the two facing the rear will now face forward. The teams go again and attempt to beat their last time.

TEACHING HINTS: Remind the players not to put their hands under the mat when they are pushing or pulling. Encourage them to work together by using a cadence to move the mat.

VARIATIONS: Place an extra cone halfway for each team. This cone also has to be circled, both going and returning.

   Have the players push or pull only one way and switch before returning.

I LOST MY PADDLE, *(cont'd.)*

Major Challenge. In this race the players change each time they go around a cone. The object is to see how long it takes all the teams to return to their original positions. Teams rotate to the cone on their right after passing the cone on the starting line. The teams passing the far right cone will stay behind that sideline and go around the cone on the far left, continuing from there.

I'M BUSHED

OBJECTIVE: To be the first team to have all its players run the course three times. (You can also time this and have them go again.)

EQUIPMENT: Twenty-four cones, six hurdle inserts, eight chairs, twelve tires, four mats and scooters

SKILLS: Running, jumping, pushing, and carrying

ORGANIZATION: Four teams, with six players on each team, line up along one sideline. Place a cone twenty feet in front of each team. The other cone is to the left of the first player lying on the sideline. The first hurdle is fifteen feet from this sideline, with the other two hurdles spaced five feet apart. Ten feet past the last hurdle are two tires spaced two feet apart. Two chairs holding the mat are ten feet from the far sideline. The third cone is also placed on this sideline and in line with the corner of the mat. Place a scooter and tire next to this cone. The first player on each team starts the game lying on his or her back with the head facing the far sideline.

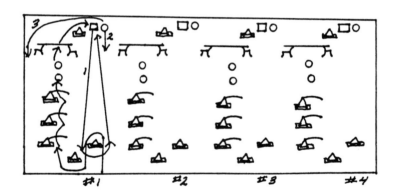

HOW TO PLAY: On a signal, the first player runs around the far cone and back around the near cone, jumps the three hurdles, steps into the tires and goes under the mat and around that cone. He or she will push the scooter around the cone in front of the team and back, placing it on the sideline. The player will then carry the tire, running the same course as with the scooter. The tire is placed on the sideline and the player returns, running to the right of the mat and hurdles. The next player in line may leave when the preceding player has started carrying the tire. Any player knocking over a hurdle or the mat has to replace it and jump over or crawl under it again before continuing. Players may have help to set up the mat. Any player failing to go around the far cone when pushing the scooter or carrying the tire has to return and do it correctly.

I'M BUSHED, *(cont'd.)*

TEACHING HINTS: Remind the players that speed doesn't always win a race. For safety, the players must stay in their own area when they are pushing the scooters. Do not allow players to step into the tire to carry it. If a player falls, the back of the tire can come up and hit the player in the head.

VARIATIONS: Players can dribble a basketball around the far cone instead of pushing a scooter.

All four teams start this race going to the left of the first team's obstacles, around the far cone, and returning between the first and second team's obstacles. They next run around the cone on the sideline by team 2 and back between the second and third team's obstacles. Players continue running around the far cone and back between the third and fourth team's obstacle. Teams finish by running to the right of team 4's obstacles, around the far cone, and behind the other team's cones until they reach their own cone. Players will stay to the right of their own cone and return to the starting line, staying to the right of the obstacles.

IT'S A STRIKE

OBJECTIVE: To see how many times a pin can be knocked down in five minutes

EQUIPMENT: One bowling pin, cone, and 7" playground ball for each team

SKILLS: Rolling a ball and running

ORGANIZATION: Eight teams with three players on each team. Each player has a number from one to three. The game is played on a basketball court from sideline to sideline. The first and third players, standing next to a cone, face the second player on the opposite sideline. Place a pin next to this player. The first player on each team is holding the ball.

HOW TO PLAY: On a signal, the first player on each team rolls the ball, attempting to knock down the pin. Immediately after rolling the ball, the player runs to the opposite sideline and either resets the pin or stands next to it, replacing the second player who retrieves the ball, returns to the starting line, and gives the ball to the next in line. This procedure is followed throughout the game. A team receives one point if its pin is knocked down by an opponent. If a pin is knocked down when a player throws the ball, goes past the sideline, or bounces the ball, it does not count.

TEACHING HINT: Remind the players not to stand directly in front of a pin and to use proper form when they roll the ball.

VARIATIONS: Play the same way, but time how long it takes the first team to reach twenty-one.

   Have every player on the team try ten times to knock down the pin. After ten attempts, the player will stand by the pin and return the ball to the next player.

JUMP THE CREEK

OBJECTIVE:	To see how many trips each team can make in fifteen minutes
EQUIPMENT:	Eighteen cones and six mats
SKILLS:	Running and jumping
ORGANIZATION:	Six teams with four on each team. The game is played on a basketball court. Two mats, on each half of the gym, are placed just outside the free-throw line. Place the remaining two mats on half-court, just outside the center jump circle. Three teams line up on each sideline, facing a mat. Each team places a cone five feet from the sideline, five feet to the right of the second cone. The second cone is placed near the sideline, ten feet from the far right corner of the mat. The third cone is ten feet behind and in line with the outside edge of the mat.

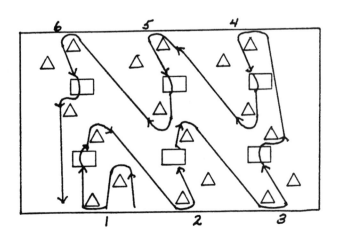

JUMP THE CREEK, *(cont'd.)*

HOW TO PLAY: The first player on each team runs the course according to the diagram. Each of the following players may leave when the player in front of him or her has jumped the second mat. Any player running the wrong way or not jumping over the mats has to go back and do it correctly before counting. Any players stepping on a mat must run around that mat before continuing. When time expires, the highest number of trips is the total to beat in the next race.

TEACHING HINTS: Make sure cones ar far enough apart to eliminate any possibility of players running into one another. Remind the players to relax when they jump over the mats.

VARIATIONS: Run the course the same way, but when a team has finished four trips the race is over.

Score so that each player passed receives one point for the team. The team with the lowest number of points either wins the game or has the score to beat in the next game.

Have each player finishing rotate one team to the right. The object is to see how long it takes everyone to return to the original position.

POOR PERSON'S POGO STICK

OBJECTIVE: To be the first team to have all players return to their original positions

EQUIPMENT: Six 18" cones

SKILL: Hopping

ORGANIZATION: Six teams with four players on each team. Each player has a number from one to four. All odd-numbered players line up on one end line. Even-numbered players line up at half-court. The game is played on half of a basketball court or similar outside area. The first player on each odd-numbered team is holding the cone.

HOW TO PLAY: On a signal, the first player on each team places his or her feet on the bottom ridge of the cone while holding the top, and hops to teammates standing at half-court. The first player gives the cone to the second player and goes behind that line. The second player then hops back to the starting line. The procedure is followed until all players are back to their original positions. The teams go through their order two times before the race is over. The race is timed, and when results have been given, the teams go again. They attempt to beat the best time. Each time a player steps off the cone, he or she has to stop and step back two paces before continuing.

TEACHING HINT: Remind the players to bend their knees and to press their feet against the sides of the cone.

VARIATIONS: Hop backwards, but go only as far as the free-throw line.
Give points to each team based on the order in which they finish. The lowest point total after four races is the total to beat in the next race.

RIDE THE RAPIDS

OBJECTIVE: To see how long it takes each team to get all the players and the mat to a designated line

EQUIPMENT: One mat, two playground balls, and twelve to fifteen wands for each team

SKILLS: Pushing, pulling, and lifting

ORGANIZATION: Three teams with eight players on each team. The game is played on a basketball court. Each team will start on one end line and finish at half-court. The wands for each team are spaced six inches to eight inches apart in a straight line directly in front of each team. Each team will place a folded mat on top of its wands. Players must lie on the mat.

HOW TO PLAY: Players may use hands or the balls to help move the mat. The wands must constantly be moved forward and placed under the mat by the players lying in front. Any player who falls off the mat has to return to the end line and wait to be rescued. The team must then return to rescue the player. All players have to be on the mat when it crosses half-court.

TEACHING HINT: Remind the players to be careful when they place the wands under the mat and to assign each player a role.

VARIATIONS: Use playground balls, soccer balls, or scooters in place of the wands.

TIRE ACTIVITIES

OBJECTIVE: To accomplish all tasks as quickly as possible

EQUIPMENT: Eight tires and an equal number of cones

SKILLS: Rolling, carrying, crawling, hopping, pulling, pushing, and lifting

ORGANIZATION: Eight teams with three players on each team. The game is played on a basketball court, with teams lining up along one sideline. A cone is placed in front of each team on the opposite sideline.

HOW TO PLAY: Give each team a card listing the following order of tasks:

1. Roll a tire with the right hand to the opposite sideline and return using the left hand.
2. Carry a tire across and back.
3. Push a tire across and back.
4. Roll a tire across and jump over it five times; return and jump over it five times again.
5. Crawl through a tire held by a teammate, going across and back.
6. Have two players, each placing one leg inside the tire, and pulling it across and back.
7. Have three players doing the same thing as in exercise 6.
8. Hook toes inside the tire and hop to the cone and back.
9. Dribble a ball while rolling a tire.
10. Tie two tires together and pull them with a 6' jump rope from one sideline to the other.
11. Push one tire while pulling another tire by hooking the toes inside it.
12. Perform combinations, such as rolling a tire to a marker, stepping inside, and pulling it over the head before returning.
13. Scoop up a basketball placed midway between both sidelines with one hand, dribble it to a tire placed on the opposite sideline, and bounce it inside the tire five times before returning the ball to the midway point.

Only the players involved may touch a tire, and for safety, each player must be sure to stop the tire before giving it to the next in line.

TEACHING HINT: Remind the players to bend their knees and to keep their backs straight when they pick up a tire.

VARIATION: Do these activities with partners holding hands.

WHO NEEDS A CAR?

OBJECTIVE:	To be the first team completing all the challenges
EQUIPMENT:	Two cones, two tires, and one basketball for each team
SKILLS:	Pushing, rolling and carrying
ORGANIZATION:	Six teams with four players on each team, each team having a number from one to six. Place two cones ten feet apart and ten feet from each corner of a basketball court. Two cones are also placed along each sideline by half-court. Teams are in a file formation along the end lines and sidelines.

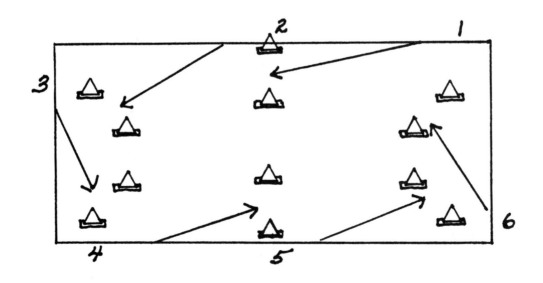

WHO NEEDS A CAR?, *(cont'd.)*

HOW TO PLAY: Each team is given a piece of paper listing the challenges. The first player, facing the set of cones on his or her right, will leave on the signal to start the race. A player's turn is over when he or she has gone between all six sets of cones and given the tire to the next in line.

The tasks to be completed are:

1. Roll the tire between all the cones.
2. Carry the tire.
3. Push the tire.
4. Roll the tire . . . dribbling a basketball
5. Jump over the tire three times between sets of cones.
6. Have two players, each putting one leg inside the tire, carry it around the course.

When the player in front has passed the third set of cones, the next player may leave. Any player knocking down a cone must replace it before continuing. Any player running into anyone has to pay a penalty, such as stepping inside the tire and pulling it over his or her head and dropping it before continuing.

TEACHING HINTS: For safety, use a tire based on the size and strength of the players. Never allow only one player to step inside to carry or pull the tire. If a player falls, the back of the tire can come up, hitting the player on the back of the head.

VARIATIONS: Play where teams one and four, two and five, and three and six, go between one another's cones while performing the tasks. It gets interesting in the middle of the gym.

Make it a cooperative race; have each player finishing go to the team to the right instead of to his or her own team. The tire is given to the next player waiting in that line. Players continue this format until all players return to their original positions. This is timed.

SECTION 5

SCOOTER ACTIVITIES,

OR,

"POOR PERSON'S ROLLS ROYCE"

ALLIGATOR ALLEY

OBJECTIVE: To get both teams across "Alligator Alley" to any sideline, using the tires

EQUIPMENT: Six tires, twelve scooters, and two mats. Six fleece balls are needed for each team

SKILLS: Lifting, pulling, throwing, and jumping

ORGANIZATION: Four teams with six player on each team. Place the two mats, joined together, in the middle of the gym. Two teams, each with three tires and six fleece balls, will stand on separate mats. The players on the two teams (alligators) surround the island, lying on the scooters.

HOW TO PLAY: Once the game starts, the players on the island must figure out how to get to the sideline, using the tires, without being tagged by an alligator. Any player falling or stepping off a tire has to run around the island before returning to the tires. Any player tagged by an alligator has to return to the island and wait to be rescued. The fleece balls are used to eliminate alligators. Once a team has used all six fleece balls, its protection is lost. The teams have to reach a sideline before time expires – ten minutes is recommended. At the end of ten minutes, the alligators and those on the islands switch places. After both teams have had a turn, they go again, attempting to beat their time. Any alligator hit by a fleece ball is out of the game and goes to the sideline until tagged by another alligator. Then he or she may re-enter the game. If one team successfully crosses "Alligator Alley," it may assist the other team, but must be on the tires.

ALLIGATOR ALLEY, *(cont'd.)*

TEACHING HINTS: Remind the players when lifting anything heavy to use their legs and not their backs. Encourage players to use the fleece balls only when absolutely necessary.

VARIATION: Have one player be the expert "marksman" and another the "swimmer" (runner) who retrieves the balls without being tagged. A swimmer who is tagged has to return to the island and be replaced by another swimmer.

OCTOPUS

OBJECTIVE:	To end up having the most goals after a set time limit
EQUIPMENT:	Four cones, four 7" playground balls, and a scooter for every player
SKILLS:	Striking, pulling, and pushing
ORGANIZATION:	Two teams with number based on the availability of scooters. Two cones, twelve feet apart, are placed on each end line. Place two balls for each team in each free-throw circle. Players are on the end line, lying on their scooters.

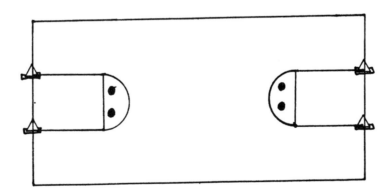

HOW TO PLAY:	Once the game starts, the players can go anywhere in the gym in an attempt to score a goal. The ball has to be hit with an open palm and rolled between the cones on the opponents' end line. There are no goalies in this game. The opposing team is given a penalty shot if any player enters the free-throw lane to protect his or her goal. The shot is taken from half-court without interference. Any team scored upon immediately puts the ball back into play. Players may not pick up a ball, get off the scooter to hit a ball, or touch anyone on a scooter. If this happens, the ball is given to the nearest opponent to put into play with a free hit.

OCTOPUS, *(cont'd.)*

TEACHING HINT: Remind the players to use teamwork by passing the ball to a player closest to the goal.

VARIATIONS: Play the same game, but with four teams. Place two cones in each corner of the gym, spacing them ten feet apart. Using a goalie in this game.

Play with four teams, adding two goals on the sideline by half-court.

PROTECT THE JEWELS

OBJECTIVE: To prevent pins from being hit with the balls

EQUIPMENT: Six pins for each team, and a scooter and playground ball for every player

SKILLS: Maneuvering on a scooter, rolling and fielding balls

ORGANIZATION: Divide the players into two teams. The game is played on a basketball court. Six pins, evenly spaced, are placed on each end line. A line, running from sideline to sideline, and five feet inside each end line, is needed to keep the players from staying too close to the pins. The players, sitting on scooters and holding balls, spread out on their own half of the court; half-court divides the two teams.

HOW TO PLAY: On a signal, the players roll their balls attempting to knock down the opponents' pins. Teams receive one point for every opponent's ball on their side, plus two points for each pin knocked down on their side. A team is penalized one point each time a player touches a ball while off his or her scooter. Return any ball rolled after the whistle has blown to stop play. If a player throws a ball or blocks one when in the restricted area, it is to be taken out of the game and counts against that team. A game is over when a team has all its pins knocked down or five minutes expire.

PROTECT THE JEWELS, *(cont'd.)*

TEACHING HINT: Remind the players not to throw balls and to be very active as they do not know when the whistle will be blown.

VARIATION: Play by the same rules, but go from sideline to sideline and increase the number of pins for each team. Place small cones, running from end line to end line, and midway between both sidelines and the center of the court.

RETURN THE MERCHANDISE

OBJECTIVE: To be the first team to take and replace all six teams

EQUIPMENT: Six scooters and hoops; seven of each of the following: bean-bags, 12" whiffle balls, hockey pucks, erasers, wooden blocks, and tennis balls

SKILL: Carrying items while lying on a scooter

ORGANIZATION: Six teams with four players on each team. Place a hoop in each corner of a basketball court and two on opposite side-lines by half-court. Each hoop contains all six of one item, such as all the erasers. The extra item is placed behind each hoop to help the players remember where each item belongs.

HOW TO PLAY: The first player on each team, lying on the scooter, will first take the item by his or her hoop before going to the other hoops and taking the same item. When the player has all six items, he or she returns, giving them to the next one in line. This player returns the items, with the last item being the one from his or her hoop. Continue this procedure until everyone has had two turns. The team finishing first establishes the time to beat for the next game. The six items have to be carried; they may not be moved along the floor. Players have to remain on their scooters when getting or replacing an item. If two scooters collide, the players involved have to return to the last hoop where an item was taken and circle this hoop before continuing.

TEACHING HINTS: For safety, have all the players move in the same direction. Remind the players that they may use any item to help carry the other items.

VARIATIONS: Play the original game, but time it to see how long it takes for all the teams to finish.

RETURN THE MERCHANDISE, *(cont'd.)*

Have the players push the scooter to each hoop, placing the items on top of the scooter.

Play the same game, but use partners when going and returning with an item. Two scooters are needed for each team; one partner sits and the other one pushes to each hoop. The player sitting then goes to the end of the line and the one doing the pushing sits on the scooter. The next in line will now push as items are returned. Continue this procedure for three rounds.

ROUND 'EM UP

OBJECTIVE: To tag as many players as possible in five minutes

EQUIPMENT: Pinnies for one team and scooters for everyone

SKILL: Maneuvering on a scooter

ORGANIZATION: Two teams with twelve players on each team. Players, sitting on their scooters, face one another from opposite end lines. Play the game on a basketball court. Each time a player is tagged, he or she receives one point.

HOW TO PLAY: On a signal, one team will start chasing the other team, attempting to tag players. Any player going out of bounds, falling off the scooter, or getting tagged receives one point each time this happens. If one player is tagged by another player who is falling off his or her scooter, it does not count. After five minutes, scores are given and the teams switch. The lowest score is the total to beat in the next game.

TEACHING HINT: Remind the players being chased to scatter, and those doing the chasing to band together as much as possible.

VARIATIONS: Play with four teams, with one team wearing the pinnies and doing the chasing.

Play with two teams, but with partners on both teams. These players hook elbows while chasing or being chased. If one of the partners is tagged, he or she goes to a designated area. When two players are in the area, they become partners. The player not tagged has to find a new partner from those who also lost a partner.

SCOOT AND SHOOT

OBJECTIVE: To score more goals than your opponent

EQUIPMENT: Twelve cones, one rag soccer ball, pinnies for one team, and scooters for everyone

SKILLS: Striking and maneuvering on a scooter

ORGANIZATION: Two teams with twelve players on a team; each player has a number from one to twelve. One team wears pinnies. The cones are used for goals. One goal, ten feet wide, is in each corner of the gym and under each basket on the end line. The first three players on each team sit near half-court; the next three are in line playing defense. The remaining six players play at goals – two in each goal.

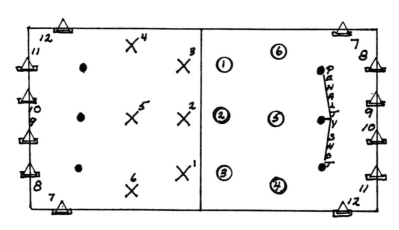

HOW TO PLAY: To start the game, the rag ball is rolled between the two front lines. Players are allowed to hit the ball only with their hands. Any ball going into a goal is immediately put back into play by either one of the goalies. A penalty shot is given when any player runs into anything or anyone. Any player may take this shot from the penalty mark fifteen feet in front of each goal. Only the goalies are involved in this play, but if control is lost any player may hit the ball. Any player picking up the ball with his or her hands gives the opposition a direct free hit. A player can score directly off the hit or pass it to another player in a better position to take the shot. Players switch every three minutes, with those on offense going to play goal – the highest two numbers going in the last goal and the lowest number helping to defend the goal under the basket. Those on defense move up to offense and the first three in line playing goal will play defense. The highest number of goals is the total to beat in the next round. When everyone has had a turn being on offense, you start the next round.

SCOOT AND SHOOT, *(cont'd.)*

TEACHING HINT: Remind the players not to grab other players, and to cooperate with teammates.

VARIATIONS: Use the same rules, but continue playing when switching players. Offensive players leaving to play goal may not touch the ball. Use two balls to play this game.

Place two cones in each corner of a basketball court and a regular hockey goal under each basket. Scoring is one point between the cones and three points when going in the hockey goal. Use the same rules, but players throw for a score. Switch offensive players and pinnies for the next game.

SCOOTER SCOOP BALL

OBJECTIVE: To score the most points in ten minutes

EQUIPMENT: One pair of goggles, a scoop, and a scooter for every player
                   Two 12" whiffle balls, four hoops, and twelve pinnies

SKILLS: Throwing and catching

ORGANIZATION: Four teams with six players on each team. Place a line midway between the sidelines, running the length of the gym. Two teams play on each side of half-court. Five feet on either side of half-court is a buffer zone. The line running the length of the gym is the new half-court line for each game. Hang a hoop from each basket on the sidelines. Each team will defend one of these hoops. Players number off from one to six; the first three players go on offense and the next three on defense.

SCOOTER SCOOP BALL, *(cont'd.)*

HOW TO PLAY: One team, designated by a coin flip, puts the ball in play. Players on offense may go anywhere while those on defense have to remain behind half-court. One team on each court will wear pinnies. One player on defense starts the game by attempting to pass the ball to an offensive player who attempts to throw the ball through the opponents' hoop. Each basket is worth one point. Any player missing a shot and catching the rebound has to pass the ball to another teammate before another shot can be taken. Each time a team scores, a defensive player on the team scored upon puts the ball back into play. A penalty shot is given any time a player touches someone in the act of shooting. This throw is taken from a mark just inside the half-court line. This throw may be taken by anyone. A thrown ball may either be caught on a fly or picked up off the floor with the scoop. A direct free throw is given to the opposition any time a player uses hands to pick up the ball to place it in the scoop. This throw can be taken by any offensive player and he or she can throw directly on goal or throw it to another teammate who may be in a better position. Any ball entering the buffer zone is given to the opposition to put in play. There are no out of bounds anywhere else. After five minutes, switch positions and sides; every ten minutes, start a new game. Have the teams that have not played one another do so the last ten minutes.

TEACHING HINT: Remind the players to use a snap throw when using the scoop. (This is a throw using mostly the wrist.)

VARIATIONS: Play by giving one point for catching a thrown ball and two points for making it through the hoop.

Give each team a ball, using the same rules, or have the teams on each sideline compete against one another.

SCOOTER VOLLEYBALL

OBJECTIVE: To be the team scoring the most points after ten minutes

EQUIPMENT: Four standards, two nets, two balls, and a scooter for every player

SKILLS: Throwing, catching, setting, and bumping

ORGANIZATION: Four teams with six players on each team. Two teams, sitting on scooters, face each other on opposite sides of the net. Two games are played at the same time. Each game is for fifteen points only, even if it is tied at fourteen. The net is five feet high on each court.

SCOOTER VOLLEYBALL, *(cont'd.)*

HOW TO PLAY: One team starts the game with a serve, which can be thrown or hit over the net. The "serving line" is fifteen feet from the net and the serve can be taken from anywhere behind this line. The serve has to clear the penalty area six feet on either side of the net. Any ball caught has to be self-set and immediately hit over the net or to teammates. Players have only one serve and must rotate to their right whether the serve is good or bad. Back-line players may not pass front-line players to play the ball. A loss of serve or point occurs when a player hits the ball twice in a row (unless first touched by another player) or out of bounds, falls off the scooter while holding the ball, enters the penalty area to hit or catch a ball, fails to return a ball on team's third hit, or holds the ball for more than three seconds. After each game the teams rotate one court to their right.

TEACHING HINT: Remind the players to keep hands out from under their scooters and, when serving, to keep the ball slightly to one side.

VARIATIONS: Any player hitting the ball over the net changes places with the player catching the ball on the opposing team. The object of this game is for each team to switch sides and return. This is timed and teams attempt to better their time.

See how long both teams can keep the ball in play using only a forearm pass or an overhead pass.

SNAIL'S PACE

OBJECTIVE: To be the team completing the most trips in ten minutes

EQUIPMENT: Sixteen scooters and cones

SKILLS: Pulling and pushing

ORGANIZATION: Eight teams with three players on each team. Play the game on a volleyball court. Teams are in file formation on one sideline.

HOW TO PLAY: On a signal, the first player on each team, kneeling on his or her scooter and using the cone, will pull to the opposite sideline and push himself or herself back. The next in line may leave when the player in front has reached the opposite sideline. This procedure is continued until players are told to stop. Players may not use their hands to touch the floor. Both knees must be on the scooter and the cone must be held in an upright position. Players receive one point each time they pass their own starting line. Total the scores for all the teams and have them attempt to beat their own score.

TEACHING HINTS: Remind the players not to throw a cone, slide the scooter to the next in line, or overextend themselves when placing the cone. The scooter may tip over, injuring their knees.

VARIATIONS: Instead of a cone, use a 7" playground ball, 16" softball, basketball, soccer ball, or football to help pull and push.

Have two players go at the same time, with one pulling and the other one pushing on the cone. Both players have to keep both hands on the cone when they play this variation.

TORPEDO

OBJECTIVE: To avoid getting hit with a rolling ball while on a scooter

EQUIPMENT: Twenty playground balls, four pinnies, and a scooter for every player

SKILLS: Rolling a ball and maneuvering while on a scooter

ORGANIZATION: Two teams with twelve or more on each team. The game is played on a basketball court, with teams facing each other from opposite end lines. Half-court divides the two teams. Two players on each team, wearing pinnies, are the "medics." Ten balls are given to each team. Players start the game sitting on their scooter.

HOW TO PLAY: Once the game starts, the players may move anywhere on their own side of half-court. If a player or scooter is hit with a rolling ball, that player has to sit by his or her scooter. Medics may rescue those hit by placing them on the medics' scooters and pulling them past their own end line. Once rescued, players may reenter the game. Players, including the medics, are temporarily out of the game if they go past half-court to roll or retrieve a ball, if they fall off their scooters to avoid getting hit, or if their scooters are hit. Players remain in the game if they are hit with a thrown or bouncing ball. Medics may be rescued only by another medic. When both medics have been eliminated, two other players may take their place.

TEACHING HINT: Remind the players to keep hands out from under their scooters.

TORPEDO, *(cont'd.)*

VARIATIONS: Have the medics, when rescuing players, sit back-to-back on a scooter, then attempt to stand by keeping their elbows hooked. If they are successful, the player being assisted may enter the game again.

Play with a partner. One partner will push while the other one rolls the ball, attempting to hit opposing players. Partners switch when either player or the scooter is hit. When both partners have been hit, they sit by their scooter and wait to be rescued, one at a time, by one of the medics.

SECTION 6

TEAM GAMES,

OR,

"SPORTS OF SORTS"

BASKETBALL

ALL CHANGE

OBJECTIVE: To be the first team to have all players finish the five activities

EQUIPMENT: Five basketballs, balloons, scooters, and 8 1/2" playground balls – and a box filled with extra balloons

SKILLS: Dribbling, kicking, hopping, pushing, and pulling

ORGANIZATION: Five teams with five players on each team. Players and teams number off from one to five. Teams line up along one end line and in file formation. The five activities must be completed in the proper order, going to the opposite end line and back. The next player in line may leave when the preceding player has passed half-court going to the far end line. Each team is given a card listing the order of events. The first player on team 1 dribbles the basketball. The first player for each of the four other teams will start, in number order, lying on a scooter, doing a seal crawl, hopping with a ball between the legs, and kicking or dribbling a balloon.

ALL CHANGE, (cont'd.)

HOW TO PLAY: On a signal, the first player on each team begins the first activity on the team's list; for example, the first player on team 1 dribbles the basketball to the designated line and back. The second one in line, lying on a scooter, pulls himself or herself down and pushes back. The third player does a forward seal crawl going down and a backward seal crawl coming back. The fourth player places a ball between his or her knees and, with hands on hips, hops down and back. The fifth player kicks and dribbles a balloon. The other teams follow the order on their lists. When the last player finishes, all players move up one position, with each player now doing that stunt. This procedure is repeated until everyone has completed all five stunts. Any player losing control of a ball has to retrieve it and return to where control was lost before continuing. Those on scooters may not use their feet and those doing the seal crawl may not touch their knees to the floor. A player caught doing this must return to the last line passed and start from there. If a balloon breaks, players are allowed to get another one from the box on one sideline and then continue from that spot.

TEACHING HINT: Remind the players to remain within their own area and to take their time when doing the stunts.

VARIATIONS: Make up your own activities.

Players can rotate one team after finishing with their own team. The object is to see how long it takes everyone to return to where he or she started.

BASKET BATTLE

OBJECTIVE: To have each player on one team make six baskets each round. Teams continue for two rounds.

EQUIPMENT: Four basketballs and one hoop for each team

SKILLS: Dribbling, running, and shooting

ORGANIZATION: Six teams, with four on each team. Teams line up along the sidelines and on the end lines. The first player on each sideline team stands next to half-court; the first player on an end line team stands to the team's right. Three hoops are placed on each half of a basketball court an equal distance from each team. Place four basketballs inside each hoop. Six baskets are used for this game.

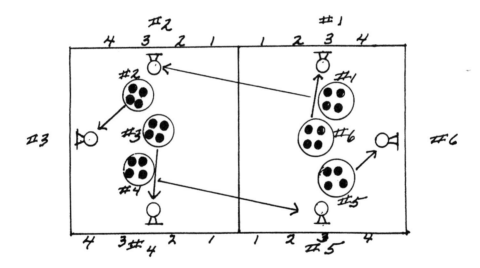

HOW TO PLAY: On a signal, the first player on each team runs to his or her hoop, picking up the ball and dribbling it to the basket on the right. The last basket made by each player is the one nearest to the player's own team. Players continue to shoot until they make each basket. This procedure is repeated with all six baskets. The next in line may leave when the preceding player makes the first basket. Any players committing a dribbling violation or interfering with another player will return to his or her own hoop and start again.

TEACHING HINTS: Place the hoops far enough apart to reduce the chance of players' running into one another. Also, remind players to concentrate on proper technique and not hurry a shot.

BASKET BATTLE, *(cont'd.)*

VARIATIONS: Players take only one shot at each basket. They receive one point for each basket made and five bonus points if they make all six.

Each hoop contains one basketball. The first player runs to the hoop, then remains behind a designated line and passes the ball to each player on his or her team. After the last player returns the ball, the first player shoots until he or she makes a basket.

One player on each half of the court receives one point if he or she finishes first.

BLANKET BALL

OBJECTIVE: To see how many baskets a team can make in ten minutes

EQUIPMENT: One towel, either a basketball or an 8 1/2" playground ball for every two players, and six baskets

SKILLS: Lifting and catching

ORGANIZATION: Two teams of two players each start at each basket. A ball is placed on the towel held by the two players. The teams rotate counterclockwise after making a basket. All six baskets must be made each round before the next round is started.

HOW TO PLAY: Partners flip or lift the ball off the blanket in an attempt to make a basket. If they are successful, they move to the next basket. If not, they remain there until they make the basket. Players may use any body part, other than their hands, to place the ball on the towel once the activity starts. Teams may go to another basket when it becomes too crowded at one basket, but only if they have not been to that basket during that round.

TEACHING HINTS: Show the players how to "pop" the towel to get more lift. Remind the players to keep their heads up and know where their partners are during the attempts.

BLANKET BALL, *(cont'd.)*

VARIATIONS: Time all the teams to see how long it takes for everyone to complete one round. Take thirty seconds off this time and have them go again.

Assign two teams to play together. The race is over when both teams have completed two rounds. This is also timed.

CAN'T MAKE UP MY MIND

OBJECTIVE: To have every player take two turns passing and receiving the ball

EQUIPMENT: Eight cones, two basketballs, and two hoops

SKILLS: Running, passing, and catching

ORGANIZATION: Two teams with a maximum of twelve on each team. Each team forms a large circle on opposite sides of half-court. Four cones are placed inside each circle to keep the circle from getting smaller while players are running. A hoop is placed in the middle of each circle. Each player has a number from one to twelve. The first player in each circle stands inside the hoop holding the basketball.

CAN'T MAKE UP MY MIND, *(cont'd.)*

HOW TO PLAY: On a signal, both circles start moving clockwise. The player in the middle, using a chest pass, passes the ball to each player in number order. When the last player receives the ball, he or she will yell, "Last" when returning the ball to the center player. The player in the middle and the second player change places and the game is repeated until every player has taken two turns. Time is given and the team goes again. Any player dropping a ball, or stepping in front of a cone or out of the hoop has to repeat the pass just made.

TEACHING HINT: Remind the players to watch the ball, not what the other team is doing.

VARIATIONS: Do a bounce pass to each player.

Do both passes to each player before going to the next one.

Have all the circle players dribble a basketball; when a player's number is called he or she exchanges passes with the player in the hoop. Circle players use a bounce pass while the player in the hoop uses a chest pass. When the ball is returned, the center player calls out another number.

CHASE OR BE CHASED

OBJECTIVE: To pass players without being passed and to finish the race with the lowest point total

EQUIPMENT: Twelve cones and twelve basketballs

SKILLS: Dribbling and running

ORGANIZATION: Twelve teams with two players on each team. If at all possible, have a boy and a girl on each team. The cones are placed according to the diagram below. Four teams are on each sideline with the other teams on the end lines. The first player on each team holds the basketball.

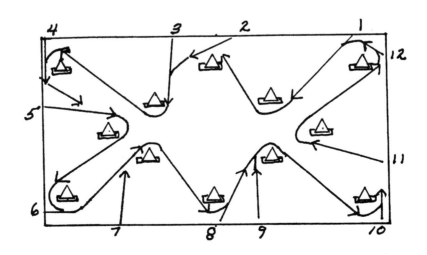

CHASE OR BE CHASED, *(cont'd.)*

HOW TO PLAY: On a signal, the first player on each team, dribbling a basketball, zig-zags through the course, attempting to pass players in front of him or her without getting passed by others. The players take on full lap. The next in line may leave when the preceding player returns and passes on the ball. Each chase lasts five minutes. After each race, players rotate to a new team, with the first player going to the team on the right and the other player going to the team to the left. Players receive one point every time they lose control of their dribble, go on the wrong side of the cone, or are passed by another player.

TEACHING HINTS: Remind the players always to pass to the right to avoid a possible collision, and to keep their heads up when running.

VARIATIONS: Repeat the same race but dribble a soccer ball.

Play with six teams and use either a football or a basketball. In this game, a team is in each corner of the gym, with the other two teams standing on opposite sidelines by half-court. The course is run the same way but a player, after passing where the last team is waiting, passes the ball to the next player waiting in line there, then returns to her or his own team.

Repeat the same race, but instead of passing the ball to a teammate, the player will go past his or her team and pass it to the player waiting on the next team, then go to the end of that line. The object is to see how long it takes all players to return to their original teams.

DRIBBLE MAYHEM

OBJECTIVE: To protect the ball from other players

EQUIPMENT: One basketball for every player

SKILLS: Dribbling and protecting the ball

ORGANIZATION: Four teams with six players on each team. The game is played on a basketball court. Half-court and a line running the length of the gym divide the gym into quarters. Assign teams to each quarter of the gym. Players on each team number off from one to six. The first player on each team rotates one court counterclockwise.

#4   #3

#1   #2

DRIBBLE MAYHEM, *(cont'd.)*

HOW TO PLAY: On a signal, all players start dribbling their balls, each player attempting to avoid getting the ball knocked away by a visiting player while remaining in the team's own quadrant. The visiting player receives one point each time he or she knocks a ball away from a player. The player receiving the most points after two minutes earns a bonus of three points for his or her team. If two or more players tie, all receive three points. Succeeding players repeat this procedure. The best point total is the total to beat in the next game. If a player going for a ball commits a foul or loses control of the dribble, it doesn't count. Visiting players receive one point when they knock the ball cleanly away from a player, or force a player to commit any dribbling violation, go past established boundaries, or use a hand to push the visiting player away.

TEACHING HINT: Remind the players to watch where they are going at all times and to use their bodies when protecting the ball.

VARIATIONS: Players go to all three courts but stay only one minute on each court. Scoring is the same.

Play until one team is eliminated (all players have had their balls knocked away). Scoring is the same.

IT'S A MESS. Play this game the same way, except everyone wears flags. The visiting player attempts to remove flags in a set time limit. The team receives one point for each flag taken in two minutes.

FIVE-STAR CHALLENGE

OBJECTIVE: To see how long each team can continue passing both balls before making a mistake

EQUIPMENT: Two basketballs for each star

SKILLS: Passing and catching

ORGANIZATION: Five teams with five players on each team, in a circle. Each player has a number from one to five (for five points of the star). Player 1 is holding the ball. Allow each team a few attempts to learn the pattern before adding the second ball. Player 2 passes his or her ball at the same time as player 1. The passing order is 1 to 3, 3 to 5, 5 to 2, 2 to 4, and 4 to 1. Players stand fifteen feet apart and use a chest pass.

HOW TO PLAY: On a signal, the first player passes the ball to player 3 and player 2 passes to player 4. They continue until the team makes a mistake. Any ball touching the ground or passed the wrong way requires that team to start over. Their time is given and they go again, attempting to better their score.

TEACHING HINT: Remind the players not to watch the ball they are passing but to concentrate on the other ball.

VARIATIONS: Players spread out and pass a soccer ball, football, or softball. Same rules apply.

    Have all odd-numbered players rotate one team and the even-numbered players remain in place.

GRAB AND GO

OBJECTIVE:	To have the highest point total
EQUIPMENT:	Three cones and four basketballs for each court
SKILLS:	Passing, dribbling, and shooting
ORGANIZATION:	Four teams with six players on each team. Teams number off from one to four. Teams 1 and 2 play on one side of half-court while three and four play on the other. Players on each team count off from one to six. Three cones form a large triangle with the base at the sideline. One team, on each half, is in a scattered formation, with the first player standing by the basket. The team dribbling first lines up along the sideline in number order. The first player holds a ball in each hand and the next two in line hold balls in their left hands only.

GRAB AND GO, *(cont'd.)*

HOW TO PLAY: The first player starts the game by rolling one of the balls anywhere in that half of the gym. He or she immediately joins hands with the next player in line and both of them dribble their balls, staying to the right of the cones. The first player, when returning, gives his or her ball to the next player in line (player 4), who does not have a ball. The second and third players join inside hands and these two dribble around the cones, continuing the rotation until every player has had a turn. The first player on the field, after getting the first ball from a teammate, will continue to shoot until making a basket. All the other players, in number order do the same thing until the last player finishes his or her turn. This player yells, "Stop!" The dribbling team receives one point for each cone passed until they are told to stop. If the dribbling team has gone through the order, they may start again. Teams switch, and play starts again. Those not shooting may pass the ball only to the one shooting. No dribbling is allowed for the team on the field. Any partner losing control of his or her dribble must stop and regain control of the ball before continuing. Players dribbling the ball must never release hands or go inside the cones. If this happens, they stop, go back and continue from there. If the player shooting commits a dribbling violation, the shot is taken from that spot. Teammates may help the shooter by retrieving and passing the ball to him or her.

TEACHING HINT: Remind the players to keep dribbling lanes open and to be careful when going under the basket where a player is shooting.

VARIATIONS: Every player on the shooting team has a ball; each player has to make three shots. This game starts when the first players on both teams start dribbling their balls. When the last player is finished shooting, he or she yells, "Stop!" The scoring is the same.

Use every basket in the gym. The rules for the dribbling team remain the same.

HAZARD BALL

OBJECTIVE: To be the first team to go through the entire order two times and end up in its original position

EQUIPMENT: One basketball for each team

SKILLS: Passing, dribbling, and shooting

ORGANIZATION: Four teams with six players on each team. Players count off from one to six. Teams line up in number order, spread out. The first player on each team is holding the ball. The game is played on a basketball court.

HOW TO PLAY: On a signal, the first player on each team starts passing the ball (chest pass) to the second player in line. This format is continued until the last player in line receives the ball. The ball is started back, and when the first player receives the ball, he or she dribbles in and continues shooting until a basket is made. All line players move up one position each time a player leaves to shoot at a basket. When a player makes a basket, he or she gives the ball to the first one in line and goes to the end of the line. The first team to return to its original position stops the game. This is timed and the two best times play against each other in the next game. Any player committing a dribbling violation has to return to that spot and take the shot from there.

TEACHING HINT: Remind the players to keep their hands away from their bodies when reaching for the ball and to concentrate on the ball the team is passing.

HAZARD BALL, *(cont'd.)*

VARIATIONS: Do a chest pass going down and a bounce pass coming back.

Play the same game, but the first basket receives five points, with three points for the second, two points for the third, and one point for the last. The highest point total is the score to beat. Players continue shooting until they make a basket. Their total is based on how they finish.

Make it a cooperative effort by seeing how many passes can be completed without a miss by either team in a set time limit.

Have each player finishing go to the end of the opposite team's line. From first place on the opposite team's line a player then goes to the end of her or his own line. When they are back in their original places, the game is over and time given.

HEAVY LEGS

OBJECTIVE: To be the first team to make eighteen baskets

EQUIPMENT: Six cones, hurdle inserts, hoops, and basketballs. Use 12"
cones for third grade and 18" cones for other grades.

SKILLS: Running, leaping, dribbling, and shooting

ORGANIZATION: Six teams with four players on each team. Teams are numbered from one to six. Teams 1, 2, 4, and 5 line up on the sidelines – two teams on each side. Teams 3 and 6 face each other
on opposite end lines. Players number off from one to four,
with the first player on the right. Six baskets are used; each
team is assigned a basket. Place three hoops on each side of
half-court at an equal distance from all the teams. Place a hurdle ten feet from each corner and five feet on either side of
half-court next to each sideline.

HEAVY LEGS, *(cont'd.)*

HOW TO PLAY: On a signal, the first player on each team will jump over all the hurdles, starting with the one on his or her right. After clearing the last hurdle, each player runs to the team's hoop, gets the ball and dribbles in – taking only one shot at the basket – then returns the ball to the hoop. The next in line may leave when the preceding player has cleared the last hurdle. This procedure is continued until one team makes eighteen baskets. If a hurdle is knocked down, it must be replaced before continuing. Anyone passing another player may by-pass the next hurdle. Any player committing a dribbling violation has to return to that spot before continuing, and a basket made as a result of this infraction does not count.

TEACHING HINT: Remind the players that only one player can jump over a hurdle at one time and to take enough air (jump higher) when jumping over the last hurdle.

VARIATION: Go over the hurdles twice before shooting. The next player leaves when the preceding player has cleared the last hurdle the first time around. Two balls are needed for each team. Time how long it takes the winning team to make twenty-one baskets.

IT'S A MESS

OBJECTIVE: For those wearing pinnies to pull flags from the other players

EQUIPMENT: One flag set and basketball for every player and pinnies for one team. A flag box containing extra flags is placed on one sideline by half-court

SKILLS: Dribbling, running, and dodging

ORGANIZATION: Four teams with six players on each team. The team wearing the pinnies has a player standing on each corner of the basketball court. The remaining two players, standing by half-court, face each other from opposite sidelines. The players from the three other teams spread out on the basketball court. Each flag pulled is worth one point.

HOW TO PLAY: On a signal, the players start dribbling their balls, attempting to avoid having flags pulled by a player wearing a pinnie. Any player going out of bounds, committing a dribbling violation, or using a hand to protect his or her flags loses one flag. A player does not lose a flag if it is pulled by a player who is losing control of his or her dribble. Players losing both flags may get extra flags from the flag box. After three minutes, play stops and those wearing the pinnies receive one point for each flag pulled. Any flag pulled is placed in the flag box. The three other teams take turns wearing the pinnies. The highest point total is the total to beat in the next round.

IT'S A MESS, *(cont'd.)*

TEACHING HINT: Remind the players to think how they can protect their flags from being taken and to watch where they are going, not who is chasing them.

VARIATIONS: Flags have a number on them from one to four. Players may pull anyone's flags and receive points based on the number of the flag.

Play the same game, but make it a team effort. Have each team wear different-colored pinnies so players do not pull a flag from a teammate. Give each team two flags with designs on them, such as squares, circles, or diamonds. These flags are worth ten points. Do not allow one player to wear both flags.

MAKE IT AND TAKE IT

OBJECTIVE: To be the first team to accumulate ten pins

EQUIPMENT: Five bowling pins and two basketballs for each team

SKILLS: Dribbling, passing, and shooting

ORGANIZATION: Four teams with six players on each team. The game is played on a basketball court, with a team standing in each corner. Five pins are placed on the end line next to each team. The teams line up in file formation along their sideline. The first two players on each team hold a basketball.

MAKE IT AND TAKE IT, *(cont'd.)*

HOW TO PLAY:　　The first player on each team dribbles the ball to the basket on the opposite end of the gym, taking only one shot. Any player making a shot takes one pin from the team on the same sideline but opposite end of the court. If the player misses the shot, he or she dribbles back to half-court and passes the ball to the next player in line. The player returning with a pin also has to dribble and pass the ball from half-court before placing the pin on the team's end line. A player who fails to dribble the ball when carrying the pin has to return the pin. The next player leaves when the preceding player has taken a shot. Any player committing a dribbling violation has to take the shot from that spot or return, passing the ball to the next one in line.

TEACHING HINT:　　Remind the players to look at teammates passing the ball, not at what the other team is doing.

VARIATIONS:　　Play the same way, but have the two teams on each side of half-court compete with each other. All twenty pins are needed to win this game.

　　Play the original game but a team may take a pin from either team on the opposite end to prevent that team from winning the game.

MASTER DRIBBLERS

OBJECTIVE: Sitting on a scooter, to knock the most balls away from those dribbling

EQUIPMENT: Scooters for one team and basketballs for the rest

SKILLS: Dribbling, dodging, and maneuvering on a scooter

ORGANIZATION: Four teams, numbering off, with six players on each team. Only half of the gym is used to play this game. Team 1 sits on the scooters, with the three other teams dribbling basketballs. This activity is timed.

HOW TO PLAY: The players start dribbling their basketballs, with those on the scooters chasing them. Any player eliminated works on shooting, passing, and dribbling on the other half of the gym. Stations are set up for this purpose. Any player committing a dribbling violation or going out of bounds is forced to leave the game. If two or more players bump into one another and lose control of the ball, both leave and do the stations. Any player having a ball knocked away by someone falling off his or her scooter is not out of the game. Once a time has been established, the other teams repeat this activity and attempt to beat the best time.

TEACHING HINT: Remind the players about the proper way to protect a ball from someone attempting to knock it away, and to keep their heads up at all times.

MASTER DRIBBLERS, *(cont'd.)*

VARIATIONS: Do not eliminate players. The person in charge records their names and they re-enter the game. This game is timed for three minutes. The team on the scooters receives one point for each player leaving the court to have a name recorded.

Play as in the original game, but each player still dribbling the ball when time expires receives one point for his or her team.

NO-BASKET BASKETBALL

OBJECTIVE: To score the most baskets by including sideline players

EQUIPMENT: Two cones, one basketball, and pinnies for one team on each court

SKILLS: Dribbling, passing, throwing, and catching

ORGANIZATION: Four teams with six players on a team, each team having a number from one to four. Players on each team also number off from one to six. The game is played on a basketball court, going across the width, if two baskets on each sideline are available. If not, play the game on the regular court. In either case, a cone is placed on each free-throw line. We will be using four baskets in describing this game. Five feet on either side of half-court is a restraining line. One team on each court lines up along the end line, with the other team on the restraining line. Three players from each team start the game on the court.

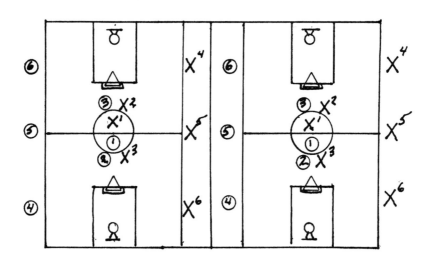

HOW TO PLAY: The game starts with one team taking the ball out of bounds. Players attempt to advance the ball by dribbling or passing the ball to teammates on the court or to the sideline players on their team. When close enough, a player may either roll or throw the ball, attempting to knock the cone over. If the attempt is successful, the team receives one point and the last player in line on the team scored upon resets the cone. The ball is given to the opposing team on any dribbling violation or foul. When a team is scored on, the ball is immediately put back in play by throwing the ball to a sideline or end line player. Players may guard anyone, and if skill permits, double-team the ball. If a player enters the free-throw circle to defend against a throw, the offensive team receives one point. If an

NO-BASKET BASKETBALL, *(cont'd.)*

offensive player enters this area to throw a ball, the ball is given to the opposing sideline. Each game lasts for three minutes; after twelve minutes the teams switch courts and the game starts again. The opposing team receives one point each time a player commits two fouls during his or her turn.

TEACHING HINT: Remind the closely guarded player that he or she has only five seconds to pass or throw the ball.

VARIATIONS: Have players rotate to the opposite team each time they switch. This movement is counterclockwise.

Play sideline basketball. Use regular basketball rules with the following exceptions: Any player committing a foul leaves the game and the next in line takes his or her place. Play for three minutes before switching. A player replacing a teammate who committed the foul remains in the game and plays with the next two who rotate in. Three players enter the game on each switch. This is a five-on-five basketball game. Each player has a number and the three with the highest number are the first to leave.

QUICK SHOT

OBJECTIVE: For one team to make the most baskets

EQUIPMENT: One basketball for every player

SKILLS: Dribbling and shooting

ORGANIZATION: Two teams with twelve players on each team. The game is played on a basketball court, with teams facing each other from opposite end lines. One team shoots while the other team dribbles the ball. Balls are placed at half-court for the team doing the shooting.

HOW TO PLAY: On a signal, the players shooting run to half-court, pick up the balls and dribble in for a shot at any basket on their half of the gym. The players on the dribbling team, leaving at the same time, dribble to half-court and back three times without turning around. The teacher or supervisor counts the baskets made until the last player on the dribbling team has passed the end line. Score is given and the teams switch roles. Play two rounds; the highest total is the score to beat in the next game. Any player committing a dribbling violation must return to half-court before continuing.

QUICK SHOT, *(cont'd.)*

TEACHING HINT: Remind the players to watch for the balls coming off the basket when shooting.

VARIATION: One team shoots for two minutes, with the other team doing a chest pass against the wall. Use partners for this game. Only half of one team will either shoot or pass the ball; the partner will record the number of baskets or passes made. The other partner then takes his or her turn. Teams switch and, after everyone has had an opportunity to do both, the score is given. One point is given for each basket and pass made.

ROTATION DRIBBLE

OBJECTIVE: To be the first player on each sideline making a basket

EQUIPMENT: Eight cones and six basketballs

SKILLS: Passing, dribbling, and shooting

ORGANIZATION: Six teams, numbering off from one to six, with four players on each team. The game is played on a basketball court. Two cones on each half of the court are placed ten feet from each free-throw line. Two additional cones are placed five feet on each side of half-court and the same distance from the center jump circle. Players are set up according to the diagram. Teams 1, 2, and 3 are on one sideline and 4, 5, and 6 are on the opposite sideline. The first player from each sideline to make a basket receives one point. Teams use a chest pass when passing the ball.

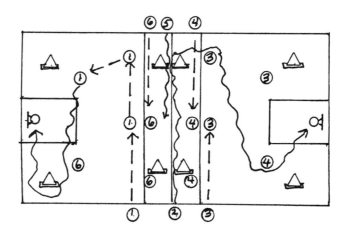

HOW TO PLAY: On a signal, the players on teams 1, 3, 4, and 6 pass the ball to one another. When the last player, on the court, receives the pass, he or she dribbles around the far cone, taking one shot. The first players on teams 2 and 5 dribble their balls around the far cone and back around the near cone before taking a shot. The other players on teams 2 and 5 wait for the whistle for the next race. Players rotate one position on the passing teams before starting the next race. Dribbling players also move up. After every player has a turn, the teams rotate to the right. Teams 3 and 6 go to opposite sidelines. Play six rounds to determine which teams scored the most points. Any player making a bad pass has to retrieve the ball and return to his or her spot before passing it again. A player committing a dribbling violation has to start over.

ROTATION DRIBBLE, *(cont'd.)*

TEACHING HINT: Remind the players not to pass the ball when someone is in front of them and to take their time when dribbling the ball.

VARIATIONS: Use the same format, except every player has to make a basket. The first player making a basket receives one point, with the rest receiving points on the order of finish. The lowest point total is the new score to beat.

Follow the same format, but have the team passing the ball go twice around before a player goes in for a shot. The dribbling team has the first player going out ten feet and pivoting before passing to every player on his or her team. The player then goes in for a shot after receiving the last pass and going around the cones.

RUN AND GUN

OBJECTIVE: To be the first team making twenty-one baskets, or to have the most baskets after a set time limit

EQUIPMENT: Four basketballs and one cone for each team

SKILLS: Dribbling, passing, and shooting

ORGANIZATION: Four teams with six players on each team, with each team assigned one corner of a basketball court. Place two cones on each half of the gym midway between the sideline and the free-throw line. Teams 1 and 3 go to the left of all the cones and teams 2 and 4 go to the right. The first three players on each team are holding balls.

RUN AND GUN, *(cont'd.)*

HOW TO PLAY: The first player on each team dribbles his or her ball around the four cones before taking a shot at the basket. That player retrieves the shot and passes it to the next one in line without a ball. The next player may leave when the preceding player has passed the second cone. (The first cone is the one diagonally across from them on the opposite side of the gym.) Players committing a dribbling violation have to back up one cone before continuing. Players waiting for a ball must be behind their own end line and in number order. Any player leaving before the one in front has passed the proper cone has to return and start over.

TEACHING HINT: Remind the players to be alert and looking ahead when crossing in the middle of the gym, and to control their dribble.

VARIATIONS: Follow the same format, but have the players continue shooting until they make a basket. Play three rounds in this game. The time of the team finishing first is the time each team attempts to beat in the next round.

Play the same game, except players dribble twice around the cones on each turn before passing the ball to the next one in line. Time to see how long it takes or play to twenty-one points.

Follow the same format, but players stop at the free-throw line to take one shot.

Have each player making a basket rotate one team to his or her right. Time to see how long it takes one or all the teams to return to their original positions.

SNAKE CATCHER

OBJECTIVE: To finish with the most points

EQUIPMENT: Five jump ropes and a basketball for each player

SKILLS: Running, dodging, and dribbling

ORGANIZATION: Five teams with five players on each team. Each team is assigned a number from one to five. Players must remain within the confines of a basketball court, or comparable area. Team 1 starts the game holding the ropes.

HOW TO PLAY: On a signal, the players holding the ropes start running around the basketball court, holding the ropes between their index fingers and thumbs. The other players, dribbling a basketball, attempt to step on one of the ropes to pull it free. If successful, the player stepping on the rope receives one point. The one holding the rope picks it up and continues running. Players have to be in control of their dribble when they step on a rope. Any player committing a dribbling violation has to leave the game and complete ten chest passes against any wall before reentering the game. If a player is caught holding the rope with a clenched fist, five points are taken away from the team's total. After five minutes, play stops and the team total is given. The other teams take their turns, attempting to beat the best score.

SNAKE CATCHER, *(cont'd.)*

TEACHING HINT: Remind those running with the ropes to watch where they are running, and those dribbling the basketball to keep their heads up.

VARIATIONS: Assign partners, with one holding a rope and the other one dribbling the basketball. When the rope is pulled free, they switch positions. When both have had the rope pulled free, they receive one point and start again.

    Play the same game, but with three on each team – two dribbling the basketball and one holding the rope. Scoring is the same.

TAKE THREE

OBJECTIVE: To be the first team to complete the four rounds

EQUIPMENT: Three basketballs and hoops for each team

SKILL: Running

ORGANIZATION: Six teams, with four on each team, line up along one end line. Fifteen feet in front of each team is a passing line. The hoops and balls are placed twenty feet apart, starting ten feet from this line and in a straight line. A bounce pass is used to return the ball to the next in line.

HOW TO PLAY: The first player on each team runs to the first hoop, picks up the ball, and returns by dribbling the ball to the passing line, where a pass is made to the next in line. The first player repeats this procedure, going to the second and third hoops. The following players leave when the player in front has either taken or placed the ball in the second hoop. The second player waiting in line always holds the balls for the next runner. Any ball not remaining in the hoop has to be replaced by that player before continuing. If a player fails to do the bounce pass or crosses the passing line, he or she has to dribble the ball around the far hoop and return before continuing. Once a team has completed four turns, time is given and the team goes again, attempting to beat this time.

TEACHING HINT: Remind the players to make sure the next player is looking before they pass the ball.

TAKE THREE, *(cont'd.)*

VARIATIONS: Have each player finishing rotate one team to his or her right. Players continue doing this until they return to their original places in line. Once again this is timed.

Have players use only right hands to dribble the ball when they are going to the odd-numbered hoops.

Play the same game, but have players dribble and pass a soccer ball.

Have the players make a basket before placing a ball in the hoop or passing it to the next in line.

TWO-ON-TWO

OBJECTIVE: To score the most points

EQUIPMENT: Four basketballs

SKILLS: Dribbling, passing, shooting, guarding, and rebounding

ORGANIZATION: Twelve teams with two players on each team. Match the players as evenly as possible by height and playing ability. Half-court divides the two courts and five feet on either side is the buffer area. The game is played on a regular basketball court, using the side baskets. Midway between each basket, on each court, is another buffer area. Two teams, on each side of the buffer area, play, with the third team standing in this area. Assign a number to each of the four courts. Teams 1 and 2 on court 1, with the third team waiting. Teams 4 and 5 play on court 2, with team 6 waiting, and court 4 has teams 10 and 11 playing, with 12 waiting. Court 3 has teams 7 and 8 playing, with team 9 waiting. A coin flip determines which team has possession to start the game. Teams waiting always start out playing defense.

TWO-ON-TWO, *(cont'd.)*

HOW TO PLAY: The game starts when one defensive player passes the ball to any offensive player. The defensive team attempts to prevent the offensive team from scoring by forcing them into a turnover. If the offensive team scores, the team waiting to play replaces the defensive team. If a turnover occurs, the defensive team goes on offense, with the team waiting, once again, going on defense. The team leaving the game goes to the buffer area. The games on each court are five minutes, with the team having the greatest point differential rotating to the next highest court and waiting in the buffer area. A player fouled in the act of shooting is given credit for a basket, and the defensive team involved has to leave the court. Any team committing a second, non-shooting foul during their play must also leave the court. If an offensive player can grab the team's own rebound, he or she may shoot or bring it out to start play again. The team on defense continues to play defense. There is no out of bounds under the basket – only on the sidelines.

TEACHING HINT: Remind the players to try to double-team at every opportunity, and to use screens to free a teammate.

VARIATIONS: The winning team remains on its own court, with the two other teams rotating to the next court – one going clockwise and the other counterclockwise.

Divide the players into three teams, with eight players on each team. Two players from each team are assigned to a court. The same scoring system is used.

WHICH CORNER IS OUT?

OBJECTIVE: To tag players and receive points

EQUIPMENT: One basketball for every player and four pinnies

SKILLS: Dribbling, running, and dodging

ORGANIZATION: Divide the class into teams of four and assign each team a number. The first group is "It" and will wear the pinnies. This team informs the person in charge as to which corner is designated as the penalty corner. The remaining teams are scattered on the basketball court.

HOW TO PLAY: The players, on a signal, start dribbling their balls, attempting to avoid going out of bounds, committing a dribbling violation, or being tagged by "It." Those tagged go to one sideline and inform the person in charge, who records this, then the players may re-enter the game. After three minutes, one of those who is "It" yells, "Corners!" The players remaining on the court quickly run to one of the corners, and those who are "It" tell them which is the penalty corner. "It" receives one point for each player caught. The score is totaled and the other teams take their turns. When "It" tags a player, he or she must be in control of the dribble, or it does not count.

TEACHING HINTS: Remind the players not to run if they are not being chased, but to continue dribbling their balls. Encourage the players to look where they are dribbling, not at who is chasing them.

VARIATION: Do not keep score. Have the players attempt to knock the ball away from any of those who are "It." If a player is successful, these two change places. The object is to see how long a player can continue to be "It."

FLAG FOOTBALL

BEAT THE SAFETY

OBJECTIVE: For the quarterbacks to have a completed pass in each zone

EQUIPMENT: Three footballs

SKILLS: Passing, catching, and defending

ORGANIZATION: There are six teams with four players on each team. Each field measures fifty yards by eleven yards, and each zone within this area is fifteen yards by eleven yards. A rushing area, five yards by eleven yards, is in front of Area One. There are three areas in each of the three fields. The quarterback is in the rushing area, with the defender just outside this area, in Area One. An offensive player and a defensive player are in each area. The quarterback should have the strongest and most accurate arm. Offensive players should be in an area matching their ability, with Area One for the weakest offensive player.

BEAT THE SAFETY, *(cont'd.)*

HOW TO PLAY: All three quarterbacks start on whistle and have five seconds to throw the ball without pressure. The player defending against the quarterback may not rush for five seconds, but he or she may jump up and down to distract or hinder the throw. A pass completed in Area One is worth one point; it is worth three points in Area Two, and five points in Area Three. A team completing a pass in each zone receives a bonus of five points. The teams switch positions after everyone on offense has had a turn. The teams scoring the most points after two rounds rotate one field to their right. Players on offense or defense may not interfere with one another when going for the ball. If there is defensive pass interference, the play counts and the team receives the points for that zone. If it is offensive pass interference, no points are given. Quarterbacks have to remain within the rushing area or any pass completed does not count. Players on offense must have at least one foot in bounds when catching the ball.

TEACHING HINTS: Encourage the players on offense to make quick moves in an attempt to get open to catch the ball. Remind the players that no dangerous or rough play is allowed.

VARIATIONS: Rotate quarterbacks every round.

The team starting out on defense receives one point each time it successfully defends against a throw.

BROKEN-FIELD RUNNER

OBJECTIVE: To have all team players return to their original positions after centering and running a slalom course

EQUIPMENT: Twelve cones and four footballs

SKILLS: Centering and running

ORGANIZATION: Four teams with six players on each team. Three cones are needed for each team. The players are ten feet apart and in file formation. The first player on each team, holding the football, stands five feet behind the first cone. The ball is centered between the legs to the next player in line.

HOW TO PLAY: On a signal, the first player on each team centers the ball to the next one in line. All the players continue this procedure until the last player in line has the ball. This player runs to the left of the first cone, to the right of the second cone, to the left and around the third cone before returning and standing behind the first cone. Players move back one position each time a player is running the course. Repeat the procedure until everyone has had a turn. Any player dropping a centering pass has to return it to the passing player and attempt it again. Any player running the wrong way has to stop and do it correctly.

TEACHING HINT: Remind the players of the proper way to carry a football, and to be ready when the ball is being centered.

BROKEN-FIELD RUNNER, *(cont'd.)*

VARIATIONS: Players can dribble a soccer ball or basketball when running the course.

Time the activity, and when the last team is finished, give the time and have them attempt to beat it.

Have each final player move to the team on the right. The object is to eventually return to the original place. This is a group challenge.

FLAG POMPON

OBJECTIVE: For one team to take the most flags after ten minutes

EQUIPMENT: One flag set for every player—different colors for each team, extra flags and a box, and four cones

SKILLS: Running and dodging

ORGANIZATION: Two teams with ten or more per team. The game is played on a field measuring eighty yards by forty yards. Two cones are placed twenty yards from each goal line and along opposite sidelines. A coin flip determines which team will go first.

FLAG POMPON, *(cont'd.)*

HOW TO PLAY:

On a signal, the team running first attempts to reach the opposite goal line without having both flags pulled off. Players losing only one flag continue to run. After one team has finished running, the other team takes its turn. Continue for ten minutes. Any player losing both flags is temporarily out of the game until he or she replaces both flags. These flags are taken from the flag box located along one sideline near midfield. A player who runs out of bounds, uses hands to protect flags, or has a flag fall of when running for the goal line loses one flag. The flag is taken off at that spot, and the player continues from there. If any player holds another player to pull off flags, it results in a free walk for the player being held. Players taking flags from the flag box must take the same color. All flags pulled remain on the ground until time expires. Flags are then counted and the highest number of flags taken is the total to beat in the next game.

TEACHING HINTS:

Remind the players to spread out, and not to run all at the same time. Tell them it is harder to pull a flag when a player is spinning rather than running straight ahead.

VARIATIONS:

Any player losing both flags helps pull flags until one team is completely eliminated. This is timed.

Have both teams pulling flags when one team is running to the opposite goal line. After three trips, count the flags on the ground to see which team has the most flags.

FOOTBALL FRENZY

OBJECTIVE: To score the most touchdowns after ten minutes

EQUIPMENT: A complete flag set for each player and a football for each game

SKILLS: Passing, catching, running, and dodging

ORGANIZATION: Four teams with six players on each team; two games are played simultaneously. The game is played on a field sixty yards by thirty yards. Teams line up on their own goal line to start play. A coin flip determines which team throws or receives the ball. Players wear different-colored flags.

HOW TO PLAY: One team starts the game by throwing the football to the other team. The team receiving the throw has two options: Attempt to catch the ball or allow it to drop to the ground and take it at that spot. A team has a maximum of seven throws on each possession. Players are allowed to run with the ball after catching it but if a flag is pulled, the ball is given to the player who pulled it. This player has five seconds to put the ball in play. Any ball dropped by either team results in a loss of possession. If a runner is about to be caught, he or she may stop running and has five seconds to get rid of the ball. Once a runner stops running, he or she may not start running again. If a ball is deflected by a defensive player behind the defensive goal line, or if an offensive player drops a thrown ball, the ball is put in play from the defensive goal line by the defending team. A team receives one point each time it scores a touchdown and then restarts the game with a thrown ball. Each game lasts for ten minutes, with winning teams switching fields.

TEACHING HINTS: Do not allow one or two players to dominate the game. If this happens, require every player to touch the ball or rule that once a player throws the ball, hr or she may not receive a return throw from that player; it has to be passed to someone else.

VARIATIONS: Have each team play for seven minutes. After three games, the greatest point differential is the score to beat the next time playing.

Have each team count off. After the first game is played, players who have odd numbers play against those having even numbers. Those who have not played each other will play the third game.

LAST FLAG PULLED

OBJECTIVE: To be the player holding the most flags after a set time limit

EQUIPMENT: One flag set for each player

SKILLS: Running and dodging

ORGANIZATION: An unlimited number of players can play this game. Players remain in a confined area measuring thirty yards by fifty yards. Inside, use the boundaries of a basketball court. A player receives one point for each flag in his or her possession. Each game is ten minutes in length. A flag box is located on one sideline near the middle of the field.

HOW TO PLAY: On a signal, players attempt to pull flags off all the other players without having their own pulled. Players lose one flag each time they use hands to protect their own flags or run past the boundary lines. Any player holding someone to pull a flag is warned the first time and loses a flag the second time. When both flags have been lost, players may go to the flag box to get two more before continuing the game.

TEACHING HINT: Encourage players to spin when someone is attempting to pull a flag.

LAST FLAG PULLED, *(cont'd.)*

VARIATIONS: Play this game with a partner. Partners have to hold hands, and when both players have lost their outside flags they switch sides, so the other flag is on the outside. When they lose these flags, they go to the flag box, and after replacing lost flags, receive one point and re-enter the game.

Use four fields. When players lose one flag on one field, they replace this flag and go to the next field and play again. This is repeated until players have been to all four fields. Players receive one point each time they go to a new field. The same game can be played with four players on each team. Rotation is the same, but after a certain time limit, play stops and teams receive points based on which field they are on. The first field is worth five points; the second, three points; the third field is two points, and the last field is one point. Everyone starts on field 1. If a team is totally eliminated, they lose one point for each flag pulled. Each game will last five minutes.

PASSING CHALLENGE

OBJECTIVE: To be the first team to complete the three challenges

EQUIPMENT: One football for each team and eighteen cones or markers

SKILLS: Passing and catching

ORGANIZATION: Six teams with four players on each team. Each team is on a field measuring ten yards by twenty yards. Place a cone along the sidelines ten, fifteen, and twenty yards from the passing line. Three players stand in the field, behind designated cones. The player with the strongest and most accurate arm should be the quarterback.

HOW TO PLAY: The weakest catcher should line up by the first cone. The other two players also line up according to their ability, with the best at the twenty-yard cone. On a signal, the quarterback throws five balls to the first player in line. Each successful catch is worth one point. The second and third players follow the same procedure. Each player has to remain behind the cone when catching the ball; otherwise, the catch does not count. After the first round the points are totaled and the highest point total is the total to beat in the next round.

TEACHING HINT: Remind the players to relax when catching the ball and to throw the ball just hard enough for the others to catch.

PASSING CHALLENGE, *(cont'd.)*

VARIATIONS:

Everyone, including the quarterback, has to catch the ball at each cone before going to the next cone. Time this activity to see how long it takes each team to complete this task.

Give each team a maximum of twenty throws to complete all three challenges. If they do not, they receive one point for each additional catch needed to finish the challenge. The lowest total is the total to beat in the next game. No points are given when a team completes the task in twenty throws or less.

PRISON BREAKOUT

OBJECTIVE: To have the most points after fifteen minutes

EQUIPMENT: Six footballs, plus one flag set for each player—different colors for each team

SKILLS: Running, throwing, catching, and dodging

ORGANIZATION: Two teams with twelve to fifteen on each team. Field length and width is determined by space available. We play on a field eighty yards by fifty yards. Three circles, spaced ten yards apart and seven feet in circumference, are on each half of the field, five yards from each goal line. Teams are randomly scattered on each half, with one player assigned to guard each circle. The "prison area" is directly behind each goal line. Teams receive two points for each football, other than their own, and one point for each prisoner remaining behind their goal line.

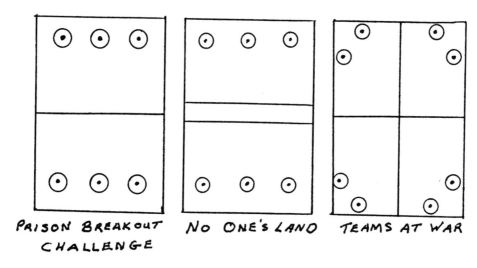

PRISON BREAKOUT   NO ONE'S LAND   TEAMS AT WAR
CHALLENGE

HOW TO PLAY: On a signal, the players from each team attempt to enter the opponents' area to get one of the footballs. If a player is successful, he or she has to run with the ball, or pass it to a teammate, past midfield without having a flag pulled. Players become prisoners when a flag falls or is pulled off the opponents' area; they use hands to protect flags; they run out of bounds to avoid getting caught in opponents' territory; or they throw the ball to a teammate who does not catch it. If it is a good throw, and one that should have been caught, the two players involved go to prison and the ball is returned to one of the circles. If it is a poorly thrown ball, it is returned to one of the circles and the player throwing it goes to prison. A player

PRISON BREAKOUT, *(cont'd.)*

does not go to prison when a flag falls off in the player's own territory. Prisoners may leave when a teammate either touches or picks up the ball; they may also take a football, but they must reach midfield without having a flag pulled. A player losing a flag must walk along either sideline to go to prison, and must hold the flag in his or her hand while walking. The game is over when the last football is carried past midfield.

TEACHING HINTS: Remind the players that they may not hold a player to pull flags, use hands to protect flags, intentionally run into a player, or dive to touch the football. Have them be aware of the score at all times. A team may end up with all the balls but still lose the game. The team with the most points is the winning team, or time the game to see how long it takes.

VARIATIONS: *Border Raid.* Play the same way, but if a team has a prisoner or prisoners, the player touching the ball has to leave the ball and take one of the prisoners. Both are allowed a free walk back if they hold hands. If not, either one can be caught. If there are no prisoners, the player may run and attempt to get the ball out of the area.

No One's Land. Use the same rules as in Prison Breakout, but there is a buffer zone between the two fields. This area is five yards wide, and anyone in this area may pull flags. The first player losing his or her flag becomes the prisoner.

Challenge Breakout. Follow the same rules, except two players, one on each side of midfield, may challenge each other without any other players interfering. These two players join hands and attempt to pull each other past midfield to pull off the other's flag. Any player assisting stops the challenge and both players are given a free walk back to their team. Players who release their grip to avoid being pulled across midfield become prisoners. If both agree, grips may be firmed.

Invasion. In this game a player may pull an opponents' flag no matter which field he or she is on. This is a wide-open game and requires complete honesty by all players.

Teams at War. Four teams play this game, with each team defending one-quarter of the field. Two footballs for each team are placed in circles seven feet in circumference, in the far corner. The game is played the same way as Prison Breakout.

PUNT AND RUN

OBJECTIVE: To score the most touchdowns after three rounds

EQUIPMENT: Four footballs and one flag set for every player

SKILLS: Punting, catching, running, and dodging

ORGANIZATION: Six teams with four players on each team. Two teams play on a field measuring fifteen yards by fifty yards. Players number off from one to four. A coin flip determines which team will go first. Two players on offense, players 1 and 2, and two on defense, players 3 and 4, start each round. Only one offensive player goes at a time; other offensive players wait on the sideline.

HOW TO PLAY: After one defensive player (3) punts the ball to the first offensive player, the two on defense attempt to pull a flag from the offensive player, who is attempting to reach the goal line. Players on defense have to wait until the offensive player has possession of the ball. Each offensive player, after finishing his or her turn, replaces the defensive player who did the punting. The second defensive player (4) kicks the ball to the second offensive player. One round is finished when each player has a turn running with the ball and being a defensive player twice. Players receive one point for each touchdown. Any offensive player who uses hands to protect his or her flag or runs out of bounds is considered caught. If a defensive player holds an offensive player running with the ball, the offensive player is granted a touchdown.

PUNT AND RUN, *(cont'd.)*

TEACHING HINT: Remind the players that they are not penalized for mishandling the punt.

VARIATION: Play three defensive players against one offensive player. Each defensive player remains within a zone (10 yards by 25 yards). The offensive player receives one point for clearing each zone without having a flag pulled. Players move up one position on every switch, and the player just finishing is then last in line. The ball is returned to the next player and he or she starts the activity again.

SIX-ON-SIX

OBJECTIVE: To score the most touchdowns

EQUIPMENT: One flag set for every player, with different colors for each team, and one football for each game

SKILLS: Running, passing, and catching

ORGANIZATION: Four teams with six players on each team. Each game is played on a field measuring sixty yards by thirty yards. Teams have four downs to score a touchdown. Each game lasts twelve minutes, with the two winning team switching fields.

HOW TO PLAY: The team receiving the ball after the kick-off may advance the ball if the ball does not touch a player first, and then the ground. If it does, the ball is put in play at that spot. If the ball is not touched by the receiving team on the kick-off and it hits the ground, any player may pick up the ball and start to run. A team has four downs to score a touchdown. If a touchdown is made, the ball is put in play for the extra point from a distance of six feet from the goal line. Extra points are made either by a pass or by a run. The team on defense has to count to five before rushing the quarterback, unless he or she rolls out, fakes, or hands off to a running back. If this happens, the defense may rush immediately. Players guilty of using their hands to protect their flags, blocking, pass interference, clipping, or holding receive a fifteen-yard penalty. All other penalties are five yards. If the kicking team is offside on the kick-off, the opposing team has the option of taking the penalty (5 yards) or starting from where they advanced the ball.

TEACHING HINT: Remind the players that everyone is eligible to catch the ball.

VARIATIONS: Do not allow running with the ball, only passing.
   Play three-on-three.
   Have the quarterback start each play holding the ball and yelling, "Hut!"

TRY TO CATCH ME

OBJECTIVE: To have more players remaining in the game after a set time limit

EQUIPMENT: One complete flag set for each player, with different colors for each team, plus four cones

SKILLS: Running and dodging

ORGANIZATION: Two teams with twelve or more players on each team. The game is played on a wide-open field. A prison, measuring twenty feet by twenty feet, is placed on one side of the field, ten yards from the boundary line. Use the four cones to mark the boundaries of the prison. One team, when it is decided which team will go first, has a thirty-second head start. A minimum of three guards should protect the prison.

TRY TO CATCH ME, *(cont'd.)*

HOW TO PLAY: Once the game starts, the team guarding the prison attempts to pull flags from as many players as possible. A player pulling a flag may take only one flag from a player and must then return this flag for the player to hold. When players lose both flags they have to hold them in their hands and walk to prison. Once a player is in prison, both flags may be replaced. Players in prison may be rescued by anyone on their team when this player runs through the prison without getting caught and yells, "Try to catch me!" If a player is holding both flags in his or her hand, and puts them back on to rescue teammates from prison, the player is considered caught, and all those being rescued must return to prison. If it happens a second time, the team committing the violation has one minute less time in which to capture the other players.

TEACHING HINTS: Remind the players not to use their hands to protect their flags or grab someone when pulling flags. Encourage them to use strategy when playing this game. For example, one player could pretend to run through the prison to distract the guards while a teammate approaches from another direction.

VARIATIONS: Wear pinnies. Any player caught becomes a prisoner and walks to prison with hands behind her or his neck.

Use nerf ball to throw at those being chased. Players hit, from the waist down, become prisoners. Any player catching a thrown ball may use this ball in exchange for a prisoner. The minimum number of balls should be eight.

FLOOR HOCKEY

FOUR TIMES THE FUN

OBJECTIVE:	To see which team can finish first
EQUIPMENT:	Four of the following: pucks, goals, rubber disks, and cones. Every player has a hockey stick.
SKILLS:	Stick-handling, passing, and shooting
ORGANIZATION:	Four teams with six players on each team, with players having a number from one to six. Each team will line up along one-half of sideline. The first player stands next to the division line, with the rest of the team lining up in number order. The last player in line is next to the end line. The division line is ten feet on either side of half-court. Place two pucks on each side of half-court in the center jump circle. Four cones, two on each half of the gym, are placed half-way between the division line and half-court. Two goals, on each half of the gym, are placed ten feet from the end line and close to each team.

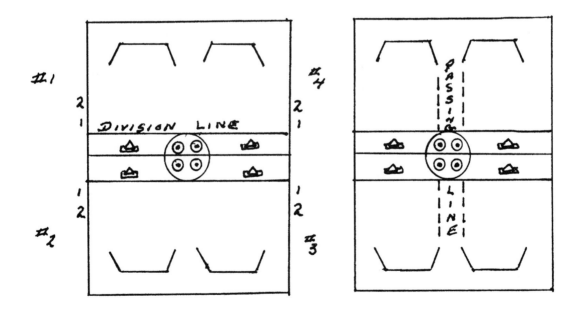

FOUR TIMES THE FUN, *(cont'd.)*

HOW TO PLAY: *Relay 1.* When a number is called, that player runs to get her or his puck, and stick-handles around the cone nearest his or her team, then down around the team's goal for either a left or right wraparound shot. If a player misses this shot, he or she must stick-handle around the cone before taking another shot. The player has to make the shot before returning the puck to the center jump circle. The other players repeat this procedure.

Relay 2. Begin as in game 1, but after going around the cone, the player must pass the puck to teammates while remaining behind a passing line. The player doing the passing moves down the line as the pass is being made. When the last player returns the puck, the first player then stick-handles around the cone nearest the team taking a "slap shot" from behind the division line. Whether the shot is made or missed, the player retrieves the puck and returns it to the center jump circle before going to the end of the line. Players move up one position each time a player leaves. The other players follow the same format. The object is to be the first team to make twenty-one goals. If any pass fails to make it to a sideline player, the player making the pass has to retrieve it and return before attempting another pass. You can also require the player to make the shot before returning the puck to the center jump circle.

FOUR TIMES THE FUN, *(cont'd.)*

Relay 3. Same as 1, but after getting the puck, the player stick-handles (zig-zag) through his or her own team before taking a wraparound shot.

Relay 4. Same beginning as relay 1, but after getting the puck, the player shoots at the opponents' goal before shooting at the team's own goal. Players continue to shoot until a goal is made before going to the next goal. Any type of shot can be taken and from anywhere on the team's half of the court. Players do not have to return and go around their own cone when missing a shot.

Relay 5. Same beginning as 1, but after passing the team's cone, players take a slap shot, retrieve the puck, and pass it to the next player waiting in line by the division line. Players move up one position each time a player leaves.

TEACHING HINT: Remind the players not to high-stick when taking any of the shots. In high-sticking, the blade of the hockey stick is above the waist on the back-swing or follow-through.

VARIATIONS: Have players on one-half of the gym work together. Total their scores to see which side had the most goals in a set time limit.

Rotate teams clockwise after each round. After four rounds, when you ask which side had the most goals, they will all raise their hands.

GOALS

OBJECTIVE: To score the most goals

EQUIPMENT: One scooter for every player, six 12" whiffle balls, two cones, and one small "pillo polo" for every two players. Safety goggles are needed for every player.

SKILLS: Passing, shooting, and working cooperatively

ORGANIZATION: Unlimited numbers divided into pairs. Each pair places the two cones (goals), spaced five feet apart, along any sideline or end line. Goals must be a minimum of fifteen feet from one another. One partner sits on both scooters, with the other player doing the pushing.

HOW TO PLAY: On a signal, the six balls are rolled into play. Players leave their goals and attempt to knock the ball into any goal while protecting their own goal. The pillo polo must not be raised above shoulders before or after hitting the ball. Players have to be on the scooters when they hit the balls. Players are allowed to stick-handle to get open for a shot on goal. Warn any player who hits the ball while off the scooters, takes hands off the player he or she is pushing, or pushes a player into anything or anyone. Penalize the team one goal each time it happens again.

TEACHING HINT: Remind the players that there is a time to be aggressive and a time to stay and play defense.

VARIATIONS: If there are enough pillo polos, give two to each player on the scooters. Use the same rules.

Play in groups of three, with one player being in the goal. Players switch after every goal.

IT'S A BLAST

OBJECTIVE: To score the most goals

EQUIPMENT: Four goals, one hockey stick for every player, and one puck

SKILLS: Stick-handling, passing, shooting, and playing defense

ORGANIZATION: Two teams with twelve players on each team. Divide each team into four groups with three players in each group. Group 1 (offense) lines up at half-court, with the two middle players facing off. Group 2 (defense) has the first and third players in the goal with the second player being the lone defender. Group 3 is on the sideline on their own half of the gym, with group 4 on the opposite sideline on the opponents' side of the gym. There is a free zone between the sideline players and the players on the field. Anyone can play the puck in this area. Two goals are placed on each end line, with the front edge of the goal on the end line. Play the game on a basketball court.

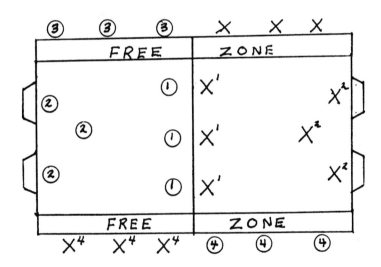

HOW TO PLAY: After the face-off any player, on the sideline or on the court, may shoot a goal. Each group plays for three minutes before switching. On the switch, team 1 takes the place of team 4. Team 4 replaces team 3, which goes on defense, and team 2 plays offense. Continue this rotation throughout the game. Any player guilty of high-sticking (the stick above the waist on the back-swing or follow-through), checking, going offside (defense going past half-court), or engaging in any rough play receives a two-minute penalty. A player receiving three penalties is eliminated from further competition or the opponent is

IT'S A BLAST, *(cont'd.)*

given a bonus of three goals. Any sideline player playing the puck outside the free zone, or a player on the court playing the puck past the sideline, stops the play, and the team committing the infraction loses possession of the puck, which is put in play at that spot. Goalies may not delay getting rid of the puck and must clear the puck to the side—not forward. Any player tripped by opposing player is given a penalty shot, which may be taken by any offensive player at either goal.

TEACHING HINTS: Encourage the players to stick-handle and to use the sideline. For safety, every player must wear shin guards, goggles, and gloves. Mouth guards are highly recommended, but must be furnished by the players.

VARIATION: Play with four teams. Each team protects one of the goals. In this game, one player is on offense, one on defense, and one playing in the goal. The puck or ball is dropped between the four offensive players to start the game. Rotate one player at a time, with each player moving up one position. Offense goes to the sideline, defense to offense, goalie to defense, and first sideline player to goalie. This is a very difficult game and requires both the offensive and defensive players on each team to work together. Using the sideline players is a must. Play for three minutes and then switch positions.

LET IT FLY

OBJECTIVE: To be the first team, following proper rotation of players, to reach twenty-one goals

EQUIPMENT: One hockey stick for every player and one puck for each team

SKILLS: Stick-handling, passing, and shooting

ORGANIZATION: Four teams with six players on each team. Place two goals on each half of a basketball court ten feet from the sideline. Players, in number order, line up on the opposite sideline. Place a puck on a designated mark behind each goal. A passing line is twenty feet in front of each team and the shooting line is twenty feet in front of the goal.

HOW TO PLAY: On a signal, the first player on each team runs around the team's goal, stick-handles to the passing line, and passes the puck to the next player in line. The player doing the passing then goes to the end of the line. The next player stick-handles to the shooting line, taking only one shot, then retrieves the puck, stick-handles to the passing line, and passes the puck to the next in line. Continue this format until one team reaches twenty-one goals. If a player goes past either line to pass or shoot the puck, have the player go again.

TEACHING HINT: Players must wear goggles for safety and make soft, accurate passes to the next in line.

VARIATIONS: Alternate goals on each half of the gym. When a player on one team passes the puck to the next in line, he or she rotates to the end of the line on the opposite team. The object is to have all players work back to their original places in line.

PUSH AND SHOOT

OBJECTIVE: Working cooperatively to score a goal

EQUIPMENT: Four goals, two nerf balls, scooters and safety goggles for everyone, and one small "softee pillo" for every two players

SKILLS: Striking, pushing, pulling, and running

ORGANIZATION: Two teams with twelve players on each team. Place four goals in the middle of the gym in an area measuring fifteen feet by fifteen feet. This is the goalie area. The goals are spaced five feet apart. Teams use different-colored softee pillos. Two players from each team, each sitting on his or her own scooter, defend opposite goals.

HOW TO PLAY: One player, sitting on two scooters with feet extended, is pushed by his or her partner around the gym to get close enough either to shoot at a goal or to pass the ball to a teammate. Players may not take a shot when inside a goalie area, but they may go through it to get a ball. If a player pushes the scooter into anything or anyone, a two-minute penalty is received and both players sit out. Players on scooters may not use hands to hit a ball, even if they are falling off their scooters. If this happens, a free hit is given to the closest opponent. A player may not take hands off the person he or she is pushing. Warn the player the first time, and assign a two-minute penalty each time it happens after that. After a goal, the goalie puts the ball back in play by hitting it. Players may switch positions any time during the game. Goalies switch to pushing or shooting every three minutes, without stoppage of play.

PUSH AND SHOOT, *(cont'd.)*

TEACHING HINT: Remind the players to switch quickly and to keep hands out from under the scooters.

VARIATIONS: Use the same rules, but have four teams, with one goal for each team.

Place the goals in each corner of the gym; play with two or four teams.

Place a goal under each basket and one along each sideline by half-court. Two or four teams can play.

SIDELINE HOCKEY

OBJECTIVE: To score the most goals

EQUIPMENT: Two goals, different-colored hockey sticks for each team; one puck; shin guards, gloves and goggles for each player

SKILLS: Stick-handling, passing, shooting, defense, and playing in the goal

ORGANIZATION: Two teams with twelve players on each team, each having a number from one to twelve. Teams face each other from opposite sidelines. The goals are placed in each free-throw lane five feet from the end line. The first player is to the right of his or her team and the others line up in number order. A free zone runs five feet from either sideline to each end line.

SIDELINE HOCKEY, *(cont'd.)*

HOW TO PLAY: The first three players start the game on offense, with the first player being the center. Offensive players may go anywhere in the gym, the next two players in line play defense, and the sixth player is in the goal. Defensive players must remain behind half-court at all times. Once the puck is dropped between opposing centers to start the game, it is not dropped again unless there is a penalty shot. The offended player takes this shot as a one-on-one challenge. Players on offense or defense may pass to one another or use the sideline players to advance the puck. Sideline players have the option of either passing the puck to a teammate or taking a shot at the goal. Players switch positions every three minutes, with those on defense going on offense. The goalie on each switch becomes the new center. The first two in line play defense, with the third in line playing in the goal. Those leaving go to the end of the line in number order. The sideline players move up three positions on each switch. Those playing in goal have the option of using a goalie stick or a regular one. The extra stick is placed on top of the goal. Players receive a two-minute penalty for high sticking (above the waist on the back-swing or the follow-through), checking, or dangerous play—or when an offensive, defensive, or sideline player plays the puck past the free zone. Players on the court or on the sideline may play the puck when it is in the free zone, but only the sideline players are allowed to play the puck past the sideline. A penalty shot is given when a player is tripped. Any player throwing a stick is warned the first time and eliminated from the game the second time. When the whistle is blown to change players, make sure those leaving do not interfere with the puck. Warn them the first time and give a penalty shot each time after that.

TEACHING HINTS: Remind the players to keep the goggles on at all times. Assign a two-minute penalty to any player who does not. Encourage the players to stick-handle when they have the opportunity, not just slap or push the puck. Make sure a new player is in the goal on each switch.

VARIATIONS: Play three-on-three with no goalie. The same rules apply.
  Play four-on-four, with one in the goal. The same rules apply.
  Play wand hockey, using a deck tennis ring and wands.

TWO-BALL PILLO POLO

OBJECTIVE: To score the most goals within a set time limit

EQUIPMENT: Twelve cones, two 6" nerf balls, and one "pillo polo" for every player

SKILLS: Stick-handling, passing, shooting, and playing defense

ORGANIZATION: Two teams with twelve players on each team. Players count off from one to twelve. When you are counting off for teams, alternate boys and girls. Two cones, spaced ten feet apart, are placed in each corner of the gym and under each basket on the end line. The first three players are on offense and line up by half-court. The next three players are on defense and remain behind half-court. The last six players are goalies, with two players, in number order, playing in each goal. Players play for three minutes before switching.

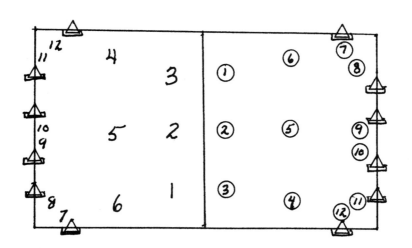

HOW TO PLAY: The game is started by rolling both balls between the two offensive teams. Players on offense may go anywhere in the gym. If a goal is scored, the ball is put back in play by the goalie, who hits it with the pillo polo. After three minutes, players switch without stoppage of play. Those on defense play offense, with the next three players (in goal) going on defense. Players play goalie in number order—the last two players in the last goal and the first player going to the middle goal. The offensive players may not touch the ball when they are leaving the court. During the game, any player guilty of high-sticking (above the waist), checking, or dangerous play receives a two-minute penalty.

TWO-BALL PILLO POLO, *(cont'd.)*

TEACHING HINTS: Remind the players to use a wall when making a pass, either to get around a player or to pass to a teammate. Tell them to follow any shot for a possible rebound.

VARIATION: Play with four goals, with each team having two goals to defend. Players line up on each sideline and rotate in one player at a time.

SOCCER

CROSS FIRE

OBJECTIVE: To eliminate opposing players by kicking balls at them

EQUIPMENT: Four or five nerf soccer balls for each circle

SKILLS: Kicking, trapping, and dodging

ORGANIZATION: Two teams with twelve to fourteen on each team. Have the players on each team count off by twos. All odd-numbered players on both teams form two large and separate circles, on opposite sides of half-court. All even-numbered players on both teams spread out in the opponents' circles. Select four to five players to start with balls. Each round is five minutes in duration.

CROSS FIRE, *(cont'd.)*

HOW TO PLAY: The players with the balls start the game by attempting to kick their balls and hit players on the inside from the waist down. Those hit go to their circle and help eliminate the other team. One point is given to each player remaining in the game after time expires. If one team loses all its players, the opposing team receives a bonus of five points. Four rounds are played to determine which team has the lowest point total. Players hit above the waist are not eliminated. Players on the outside of the circle may not use their hands to stop the ball. Any player who does must give the ball to the player on his or her right. A ball going outside the circle has to be dribbled back before any kicks can be attempted.

TEACHING HINT: Remind the players not to kick too hard, and to be good sports and admit it when hit with a ball.

VARIATIONS: Have four on a team, with two of the players inside one circle and the other two being part of another circle. When one player is hit, he or she changes places with a teammate forming another circle. When all four players have been hit, they receive one point and start over. After a certain time limit, play stops and scores are tallied. If only one player has been hit, the team receives a quarter of a point. The lowest point total is the total to beat. Those who started inside the circle start the new game forming the circle.

DOUBLE TROUBLE

OBJECTIVE: To complete five soccer passes without losing control of the ball

EQUIPMENT: Shin guards for every player and six soccer balls

SKILLS: Passing, controlling, receiving, and tackling

ORGANIZATION: Twelve teams with two players on each team. Teams count off from one to twelve. All odd-numbered teams have the ball to start the game. Place four cones in the corners of an area measuring ten yards by ten yards for each field. There are six fields, with fifteen feet between fields. Teams 1 and 2 play on field 1; teams 3 and 4 on field 2. The remaining teams follow the same format.

HOW TO PLAY: The odd-numbered teams start the game by attempting to complete five passes without losing possession of the ball. If they are successful, each team receives one point and the ball is given to the other teams to start the next game. After five minutes, the team with the highest point total rotates one field to the right, with the opponents starting the next game. Players must remain within their own area while in possession of the ball. If the ball goes out of bounds, the team committing this infraction loses the ball. The ball is put back in play within the field, not where it went out. Players may not use their hands to gain an advantage by pushing or holding an opponent, or to stop the ball. Players are allowed to dribble before passing the ball.

DOUBLE TROUBLE, *(cont'd.)*

TEACHING HINT: Remind the players to break to an open area after passing the ball, and not to wait in the same spot for a return pass.

VARIATIONS: Play three-on-three. Have the teams play until one team receives three points. These teams play against another winning team.

Play four-on-four, with one playing in the goal.

Have partners, passing and dribbling the ball, be in possession of the ball when they pass the opponents' goal line to receive one point. The goal line is the same as in the original game.

GIVE AND GO

OBJECTIVE: For two teams, working together, to properly pass the soccer ball, both going and returning, as many times as possible in four minutes

EQUIPMENT: Eighteen cones and six soccer balls

SKILLS: Dribbling, passing, and trapping

ORGANIZATION: Twelve teams with two players on each team. An area eighty yards by fifty-five yards is needed to play this game. If space is limited, reduce the size of each field. Two teams play on a field measuring thirty-five yards on the length of the area by fifteen yards on the width. Between each two fields is a buffer zone of five yards on the side and ten yards at one end. Two teams (in number order) work together. Place the cones midway between the two teams and thirty feet apart in a straight line, starting from the goal line. Each team lines up along the side-line (touch line). The first player on each odd-numbered team has the ball to start the game.

HOW TO PLAY: On a signal, the first player on team 1 passes the ball to the first player on team 2 before that player reaches the first cone. That player, after receiving and controlling the ball, dribbles the ball past the first cone before returning the ball. Players continue this format until they reach the third cone. Each player, with one dribbling the ball, circles the cone and returns, doing the same thing but using the opposite foot to pass the ball. This is continued until both players reach the opposite team. Both players will go to the end of the opposite team's line, with the next two taking their turn. Teams receive one point each time a pair finishes a turn. Only one pass may be

GIVE AND GO, *(cont'd.)*

made between the cones. Players may not use hands to control the ball. If this happens, both players return to their teams, giving the ball to the next two to go. If a cone is missed, both players and the ball have to return to the last cone passed and continue from there.

TEACHING HINT: Remind the players to use both sides of their feet when passing the ball and to remain next to their own sideline for safety.

VARIATIONS: Each time a player finishes a turn, he or she rotates one team to the right. The object of this relay is for the players to return to where they started within a certain time limit.

Have all odd-numbered players rotate one field after each game.

Use two balls for each game, with each pass being made before reaching the cones.

KICK AND SCORE

OBJECTIVE:　　　To have the lowest score after two rounds

EQUIPMENT:　　　Two hoops and holders, four cones, and two different-colored soccer balls for each field

SKILL:　　　Kicking

ORGANIZATION:　Eight teams with three players on each team. Each game is played on a field measuring ninety by forty yards. Two hoops, spaced eighty yards apart and five yards from each end line, are on each field. The four cones are placed in the corners for boundaries. A coin flip determines which team goes first.

KICK AND SCORE, *(cont'd.)*

HOW TO PLAY: Each team stands behind the starting line. The first player kicks his or her ball as far as possible, attempting to keep it in play. The opposing player takes his or her turn. After that, the team most distant from the hoop kicks first. The other players, in number order, continue this format until one team kicks the ball through the hoop. The first team making it through the hoop receives one point. Players kicking out-of-order or out of bounds receive a one-kick penalty. The ball is put in play where it went out. When an opposing player interferes with a kick, the team receives a bonus kick, without having it count against the total. The team with the lowest total after two rounds rotates to the next field on the right.

TEACHING HINTS: Remind the players to remain behind the one kicking the ball to eliminate the possibility of injury. Encourage them to work on proper kicking technique.

VARIATIONS: Play with four hoops and place them in a diamond setup.
    Use frisbees or a football to play this game.
    Have all the teams play one round and tally their score, then go again, attempting to beat this score.

KNOCK 'EM OVER

OBJECTIVE: To protect the team's goal and end with the lowest point total after a set time limit

EQUIPMENT: One soccer ball and cone for every two players, and shin guards for everyone

SKILLS: Goal tending, dribbling, kicking, trapping, and punting

ORGANIZATION: An unlimited number of players divided into pairs. Teams and cones are in a scattered formation on a large, open field or similar indoor area.

HOW TO PLAY: One partner guards the cone while the other partner attempts to knock down the opponents' cones by dribbling close enough to kick the ball. Partners change any time their cone is knocked down. The cone remains down until the guarding partner returns with the ball. When a cone has been knocked down twice, it remains down until the person in charge is told. The team receives one point and re-enters the game. Goalies may use hands and feet to protect their goal. Any player kicking a ball above the waist is given a warning. If it happens a second time, the team is penalized one point. Goalies should be encouraged to punt any balls they can control, but only away from players. Goalies may not stand on any part of a cone. A partner may help his or her goalie.

KNOCK 'EM OVER, *(cont'd.)*

TEACHING HINTS: Encourage the goalies to be aggressive and challenge any player coming near their cones. Use soft or partially deflated balls and remind players to make short kicks when they kick at a cone.

VARIATIONS: When a team has a cone knocked down twice, it remains down until one of the partners knocks down a cone. Both players may do this, but they have to share a ball.

Give each player a ball and a cone. In this game, the player has to decide when it is safe to leave for an attempted shot at an opponents' cone. If his or her cone is knocked down three times, one point is given.

MICKEY MOUSE

OBJECTIVE: To make the most trips

EQUIPMENT: Sixteen soccer balls, eight cones, and eight hoops

SKILLS: Dribbling and kicking

ORGANIZATION: Eight teams with three players on each team. The game can be played on a basketball court or large field. Six feet on both sides of half-court is a buffer zone, to separate two teams for safety. Four cones are used on each court to form one large square. Four teams are on each half of the field or court. Place four hoops in a diamond formation in the middle of this square, with each hoop being an equal distance from a team. Place two balls inside each hoop. The teams line up along both sidelines, both end lines, and on each side of the buffer zone. Players number off from one to three, with the first player on the right of the team.

MICKEY MOUSE, *(cont'd.)*

HOW TO PLAY: On a signal, the first player on each team runs to his or her hoop and, after getting the ball, dribbles it twice around the square, starting with the hoop on the team's right, before placing it back in the hoop. The next player in line may leave when the player in front has passed the third cone. Continue this procedure for five minutes. The team with the most trips on each half of the gym or field switches sides. Players may not use their hands to control or pick up the ball. Opposing players may not interfere with any opponent's ball. Players finishing a turn go to the end of the team's line.

TEACHING HINT: Remind the players to keep their heads up when dribbling the ball, and always to pass another player on the right.

VARIATIONS: Place a goal in front of each team instead of a hoop. The first player in line is holding the ball. After dribbling the ball twice around the circle, a player takes one shot on goal before giving the ball to the next player in line. Teams continue this format for five minutes. The total number of goals determines which teams switch.

Have the players, after getting the ball from the hoop, pass the ball to teammates before dribbling once around the square.

Play the same way, but have each player head the ball.

PUNT, DRIBBLE, AND KICK

OBJECTIVE: To score the most points

EQUIPMENT: Twelve cones and six soccer balls

SKILLS: Punting, dribbling, kicking, passing, and trapping

ORGANIZATION: Six teams with four players on each team. Two teams - one to punt and the other to field - play the game on a field measuring twenty yards by fifty yards. Draw two circles, five feet in diameter, twenty and forty yards from the kicking line. Place a cone in each circle. The other two cones are five feet from the sideline and fifteen and thirty yards from the kicking line. One ball is placed on the kicking line directly in line with these two cones. One player on the team in the field stands next to each of the two cones in the circles, with the other two players playing the field. The first player on the punting team has two balls.

PUNT, DRIBBLE, AND KICK, *(cont'd.)*

HOW TO PLAY: The first player on the punting team, after kicking one ball into the field, runs to the second ball on the kicking line, dribbles this ball around the two cones directly in front of him or her, and continues to do so until the other team has knocked down both cones. One point is given for each round trip made by the dribbling player. The team on the field, after the punt, has to gain control of the ball and pass it to one of the players standing by a cone. This player attempts to kick the ball and knock over the cone. If the player misses, the ball must be retrieved by one of the two players on the field—not by the player at the cone. If a cone is knocked down, the ball is passed to the other player at the second cone, who repeats the procedure. When the second cone is knocked down, play stops. The cones are reset for other players to take their turns. The teams switch and the game is repeated, with each team having two turns. Players on the field may not use their hands at any time to stop or control the ball. The player by the cone must first control the ball before kicking at the cone. If the player dribbling the ball loses control and kicks it into the opponents' area, the team on the field may kick it anywhere on the field. The dribbling player must retrieve the ball and dribble it back to where he or she lost control before continuing to dribble around the cones. The players on the field may not dribble the ball; they must pass it.

TEACHING HINT: Remind the players to control the ball before attempting to pass or kick at a cone.

VARIATIONS: The player dribbling the ball has to zig-zag through a series of cones, going down and back as many times as possible before the opposing team knocks down both cones.

  Use two cones, spaced five feet apart, as a goal. Players on the field have to kick the ball through the goal instead of knocking down the cones. Have the players remain a minimum of ten feet away to attempt the goal.

QUICK FEET

OBJECTIVE: To see how long it takes the teams to get all players back to their original positions

EQUIPMENT: Eight soccer balls and sixteen cones

SKILLS: Dribbling, passing, and trapping

ORGANIZATION: Eight teams with three on each team. Eight cones are set up five feet from each sideline, end line, and half-court. The other eight cones are placed midway between the teams. Four teams play on each half of the gym or field. The first player on each team stands to the right of his or her cone facing counterclockwise. The second and third players in line stand behind the first player, also facing counterclockwise. The ball is placed on the floor in front of the first player on each team.

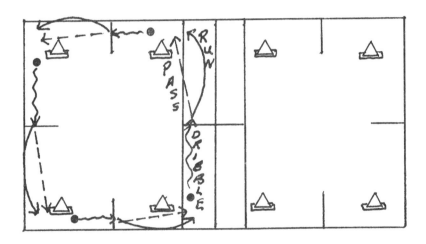

HOW TO PLAY: On a signal, the first player on each team dribbles the ball to the cone midway between the two teams. After reaching the cone, the player passes the ball to the player waiting in line at the next cone. The first player then goes to the end of that line. The player receiving the pass has to control it, dribbling, to the next cone. Any player losing control of the dribble, making a bad pass, or going past the cone when making a pass has to stop and return before continuing. Those waiting in line may not assist a teammate in any way. Players continue with this format until all players are back in their original positions after each player has gone three times. The first player on each team rotates one team to his or her right on the team's half of the gym—after the time has been given.

QUICK FEET, *(cont'd.)*

TEACHING HINT: Place two cones five feet from each team, spaced three feet apart. Each player dribbles to the cone and then has to pass the ball between the cones to the next player in line.

Have the first player dribble completely around all the teams on the team's half of the gym before making the pass from the cone midway between the teams. Use the same format as in the original game.

SOCCER LEAPFROG

OBJECTIVE: To be the first team to complete the task by having every player end up where he or she started

EQUIPMENT: One hoop and one soccer ball for each team

SKILLS: Jumping, dribbling, and trapping

ORGANIZATION: Six teams with four players on each team. The game is played on an open field. Teams are in file formation, with players five feet apart. The hoop, with the ball inside, is placed thirty feet in front of the first player on each team.

HOW TO PLAY: On a signal, the last player on each team leapfrogs over teammates, runs and gets the ball, and dribbles it back, zig-zagging between teammates. The last player is circled and the dribbling player continues dribbling the ball back to the hoop, then takes the place at the front of the line. Teammates move back one position. The next player may leave when the returning player is in the front of the line and yells, "Go!" A player may not use hands at any time to touch the ball, hinder an opponent, or move from his or her position to help a teammate who has lost control of the ball. Players start over if they do not zig-zag between the players during the dribble or if they do not lift both legs when jumping over teammates.

SOCCER LEAPFROG, *(cont'd.)*

TEACHING HINT: Remind the players to keep their heads down and hands on their knees for support when being jumped over.

VARIATION: Players can kick for a goal after dribbling the ball and before returning to their hoops. Place the goal, two cones spaced five apart, fifteen feet behind the hoop. The player has to make a goal before returning the ball to the hoop.

TWO-BALL SOCCER

OBJECTIVE: To score the most goals

EQUIPMENT: Four cones, two balls (partially deflated), pinnies for one team, and shin guards for everyone

SKILLS: All soccer skills

ORGANIZATION: Two teams with eleven or more on each team. The game is played on a field measuring 100 yards by fifty yards. A penalty area fifteen yards by ten yards is placed five yards from each end line and seventeen and one-half yards from each touch-line or sideline. The front of the penalty area is thirty-five yards from midfield. The cones are used as goals and are spaced fifteen feet apart, five yards from each side of the penalty area. Five players play on the front line, four on defense, and two in each goal. If you have an odd number of players, place the extra ones in the front line. A circle ten feet in diameter is drawn in the middle of the field. Two yards from the midfield line is a mark (staggered) for kick-offs. Only the center-forwards are allowed in this area, with each having a ball.

TWO-BALL SOCCER, *(cont'd.)*

HOW TO PLAY: Once the balls have been kicked to start play, all players may go anywhere on the field. There is no out of bounds in this game. Players are allowed to use arms to protect their upper bodies and faces. Goalies may use their hands while in the penalty area. Other players may not enter this area at any time during the game. Any goal scored does not count if this happens. The only time play stops is when a player intentionally trips another player or is guilty of charging a goalie. A penalty kick is given and the shot is taken from just outside the penalty area. A goal can be scored from either side and the ball is always kept in play. A team scoring from one side of the goal and controlling the ball may shoot on goal again. Players switch positions and sides halfway through the period.

TEACHING HINT: Remind the goalies that one player must always face the ball.

VARIATIONS: Play six-on-six, with the other players on each sideline.

Play with four teams, each team defending a goal. Goals are placed on sidelines by midfield and on both end lines or goal lines. No penalty areas in this game. Players may score in any of the other three goals and from either side. Use four different-colored pinnies for this game.

TWO CRABS ARE BETTER THAN ONE

OBJECTIVE: To score the most goals

EQUIPMENT: Twenty-four cones and twelve soccer balls

SKILLS: Kicking, catching, and maneuvering in a crab-walk position

ORGANIZATION: Twelve teams with two players on each team. The cones are used as goals. Three goals (cones five feet apart), evenly spaced along the end lines and sidelines. One partner is the goalie, with the other partner in front of the goal in a crab-walk position. Each player in front of the goal has a ball. The goalie can either sit or assume a crab-walk position. Each game lasts fifteen minutes.

HOW TO PLAY: The player in front of each goal, on a signal, attempts to kick any ball into one of the goals while keeping both hands on the floor. The player in the crab-walk position in front of the goal has the option of attempting to kick for a goal or helping to defend the home goal. Partners switch every three minutes. Goalies may use hands or feet to defend the goal. A goal is scored when it passes the goalie from the shoulders down. If a player on the field gets tired, he or she may stand up and change places with the goalie—even if the three minutes are not up. The greatest point differential (goals scored versus goals allowed) is the total to beat in the next game.

TEACHING HINT: Remind the players not to kick a ball when there is a chance of kicking another player.

TWO CRABS ARE BETTER THAN ONE, *(cont'd.)*

VARIATION: Play the three teams on the end lines against those on the sidelines. Total the points for each group of three teams. Pinnies are then needed for six teams.

SOFTBALL

CHOICE BALL

OBJECTIVE: To score the most runs

EQUIPMENT: Four bases, bats, tennis racquet, tennis ball, 7" playground ball, and one batting tee

SKILLS: Catching, throwing, running, hitting, and pitching

ORGANIZATION: Players are divided equally into two teams. A coin flip determines which team will bat first. The other team is on the field, with a player at each position. If you have more than ten players, assign them to the outfield. Allow three outs for each team or one time through the order—whichever comes first. Follow regular softball rules with the following exception: Allow any player making an out on a fly ball or failing to beat the throw to first base to run the bases and count the run, if it is made. Bases for this game are sixty feet apart. The catcher must wear a mask, and players are not allowed to slide or run into a fielder.

CHOICE BALL, *(cont'd.)*

HOW TO PLAY: The player at bat has the choice of kicking a stationary ball, hitting any of the balls off the tee, hitting a pitched or self-tossed ball, or hitting a tennis ball with a tennis racquet. A runner on base may not leave until a stationary ball has been kicked, a ball has been hit off the tee, or a pitched ball has crossed home plate. If a player reaches first base, but is thrown out going for another base (this player then gets back in line), or if the player who is up throws the bat or tennis racquet, the player at bat is not allowed to go to first base.

TEACHING HINTS: Encourage the players to remain behind a backstop if you have one. If not, have the players face the batter from a distance of twenty feet, along the foul line.

VARIATIONS: Allow five outs or going through the order one time, whichever comes first.

Play with six on a team and close one field. Two games can be played at one time. The field to be closed depends on whether the hitter hits from the right or the left side.

Have everyone bat before switching. The last player has to keep running until he or she makes an out.

Give everyone on each team a number. In the first inning, everyone on both teams bats. All odd-numbered players on both teams switch to play the second inning. For the third inning, have the remaining players switch. In the fourth inning, repeat the first inning.

CRAZY BALL

OBJECTIVE: To score the most runs

EQUIPMENT: Four bases and one 8 1/2" playground ball

SKILLS: Kicking, catching, throwing, and running

ORGANIZATION: Two teams with twelve on each team. One team is on the field, with a player at each position. Extra players are in the outfield. The game is played on a regular softball diamond. The pitcher has the ball to start the game. Two runners may be on the same base, and there are three outs per inning. Any player making an out when kicking the ball is still allowed to run the bases, starting at first base. There are no force-outs in this game, but if the ball beats any runner going to a base, he or she is out.

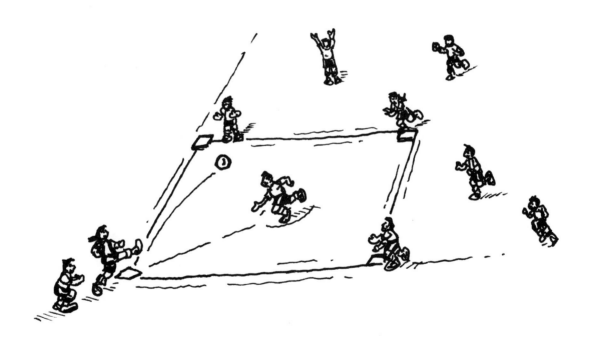

HOW TO PLAY: The first player kicks a rolled ball and has the option of running to any base. If the player kicks the ball toward third or short, he or she should run to first. If the kick is to second or first, the runner should go to third. The bases may be run in any order as long as a base is not repeated. Home plate has to be the last base touched. A player who repeats a base, is beaten by the ball to a base, or stops on a base with more than two runners is out.

CRAZY BALL, *(cont'd.)*

TEACHING HINTS: Remind the players to kick the ball as hard as possible. Penalize a team when a fielder throws a ball at a runner and hits that runner. That runner and all those going for the same base are allowed to score.

VARIATIONS: Have all the players kick before switching. When the last player kicks the ball, all the runners have to attempt to score before the one who kicked the ball makes an out.

Play with two balls, with the person in charge doing the pitching. The second ball is pitched after the first player has kicked a fair ball. The next player in line has to be ready. If the ball crosses home plate and is not kicked, the player is out. Either ball may be used to get one or both runners out.

DEEP FLY RELAY

OBJECTIVE: To be the first team to finish all the quadrants

EQUIPMENT: Twenty cones and eight 12" soft or nerf balls

SKILLS: Running, throwing and catching

ORGANIZATION: Eight teams with three players on each team. The game is played on a field measuring thirty yards by forty yards. Each area is ten yards by ten yards. Place a cone ten, twenty, and thirty yards from the starting line to separate the four areas of the field. Teams count off. Two teams, in number order, play on each field. Set each team's rotation by starting the weakest arm and ending with the strongest arm. Distance is determined by age and ability. Players on each team line up in file formation.

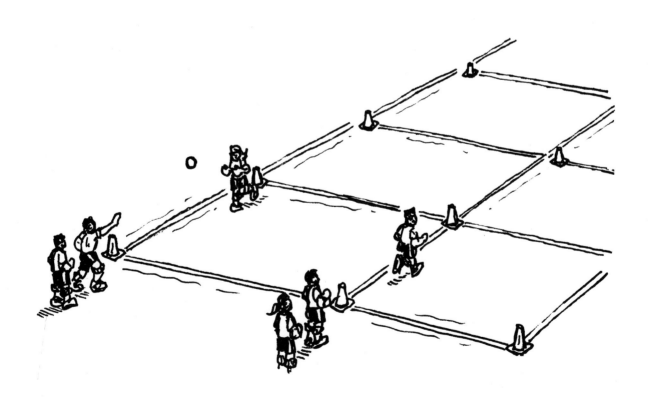

DEEP FLY RELAY, *(cont'd.)*

HOW TO PLAY: The first player on each team (weakest arm) starts the game by throwing the ball to the next player in line, who has to run to the first cone thirty feet away. This player remains at the cone until the ball is caught or a maximum of five attempts has been made. In either case, this player returns, giving the ball to the first player. The next player waiting in line repeats this procedure going to the same line, but returns the ball to the second player who repeats what the first player did, throwing to the second cone sixty feet away. Finally, the third player (strongest arm) throws to teammates ninety feet away—the "deep fly line." When the last player has caught the ball, or had five chances to catch the ball and has returned the ball, the relay is over. The ball may not be caught or thrown from in front of a marker. Have the teams finishing first on each field move one field to the right.

TEACHING HINT: Remind the players not to throw a ball until the player is looking and to use proper form when catching a ball above and below the waist.

VARIATIONS: Use a football or frisbee and play the same way.

Have four teams compete against one another, with points being given in order of finish. The lowest total is the total to beat in the next game. Have even-numbered players rotate two teams to the right.

GO FOR IT

OBJECTIVE: To score the most runs after three innings

EQUIPMENT: Bats, two batting tees, two softballs, two sets of bases, and enough gloves for the players on the field

SKILLS: Hitting, fielding, base running, throwing, decision making, and learning how to use the cut-off person

ORGANIZATION: Four teams with six players on each team. Each game should be played on a field measuring forty yards by sixty yards. The bases, starting from the batting tee, are fifteen yards apart and in a straight line. One team, except for the catcher, is on the field, with one player standing by the first base and the others scattered on the field. The catcher has to remain behind the hitting line to catch any thrown ball. The team at bat goes through he entire order two times before switching sides.

GO FOR IT, *(cont'd.)*

HOW TO PLAY: The first player, after hitting the ball, will run the bases, based on where the ball is or whether the fielders are having trouble fielding the ball. Each base a runner touches is worth one run if he or she returns before the ball is caught on a fly or on the first bounce by the catcher. If a player touches three bases and makes it safely back, the team gets three runs. A player makes an out by having a fly ball caught or going past the foul lines at either side on a fly, having the catcher catch the ball before the runner passes the hitting line, or throwing a bat. Any fielder interfering or obstructing a runner receives a two-run penalty. Any runner interfering with a throw to the catcher is out. Fielders are not allowed to run with the ball after picking it up; the ball has to be thrown from that spot. If it is not, the ball must be returned to that player and he or she has to bring it back to that spot before throwing it again. A smart base runner, seeing this, should go for an extra base before returning. Replace the catcher every inning. Any ball barely making it into the field of play has to be fielded by the catcher and thrown to the fielder by first base, who must return the throw before the runner reaches the hitting line, or the hitter gets one run.

TEACHING HINTS: Encourage the players to use the cut-off person instead of attempting a long throw. Remind them that it can bounce only once when it is thrown to the catcher. Remind those waiting their turn to hit to face the hitter and stand a minimum of fifteen feet away.

VARIATIONS: Use an incrediball baseball or 16" softball. Move the bases closer for the softball and out for the baseball.

Play the same game and use the same rules, but use a soccer ball. The player punts the ball and the fielders have to control the ball and pass it to the catcher who kicks for a goal. The goal is to the left of the player punting the ball, on the side of the hitting line. Cones should be placed five feet apart.

GOING, GOING, GONE!

OBJECTIVE: To score the most runs after three innings

EQUIPMENT: For each field you need eight cones, one softball, a batting tee, bats, and softball gloves for each fielder

SKILLS: Hitting, throwing, and catching

ORGANIZATION: Four teams with six players on each team. Two games are played simultaneously. One team is on the field in a scattered formation, with one player standing next to the first cone. Players at bat have three chances to hit a fair ball. Four cones, starting from the hitting line, are spaced every fifteen yards. These cones are in a straight line and to the left of the hitting team. Teams go through their order twice before switching. Batting order should go from weakest to strongest hitter. Each field measures sixty yards by forty yards.

GOING, GOING, GONE!, *(cont'd.)*

HOW TO PLAY: The first player hits the ball. The player advances to the first cone for a single on a ground ball that is not caught and is hit past the hitting line but in front of the first cone, as long as the player beats the throw to the fielder by this cone. Players automatically advance to first base if the ball goes past the first cone, but lands in front of the second cone. A player gets a double if the ball is hit past the second cone but in front of the third cone (as long as it is not caught). A ball hit between the third and fourth cones is worth a triple, and a home run is received when a ball goes past the fourth cone and is not caught. A hitter is out when a ball goes past the cones on either side of the field of play, or when the hitter fails to hit a fair ball after three attempts. Hitting the batting tee constitutes a strike.

TEACHING HINTS: Remind the players to advance the proper number of cones on each hit. Have those waiting to hit face the hitter and stand a minimum of fifteen feet away.

VARIATIONS: Kick a stationary 7" playground ball. Move cones closer for this game.

Wall Kicker. The first cone is twenty feet from the wall, with the other cones spaced ten feet apart. The ball to be kicked is placed fifteen feet from the wall. Rules are the same. Players have one chance to kick the ball against the wall. If the ball does not pass the first cone on a fly, the kicker is out. Strongest kickers should go last. Each team goes through the order twice before switching.

HOOP BALL

OBJECTIVE: To touch as many bases as possible before the team on the field completes its assigned task

EQUIPMENT: Four bases and one hoop for each team

SKILLS: Throwing or rolling a hoop and running

ORGANIZATION: Four teams with six players on each team. Two games are played on separate fields. One team is on the field in scattered formation, with the other team starting the game. Use a regular softball diamond, with bases sixty feet apart. The first player on each starting team holds a hoop. Foul lines are also used in this game.

HOW TO PLAY: The first player rolls or throws the hoop, keeping it in the field of play, and starts running the bases. Players on the field may not touch the hoop until it stops rolling. The closest player picks it up and holds it for teammates who go through in one direction. When the last player has gone through the hoop, the one holding it yells, "Stop!" The player running the bases receives one point for each base he or she touches before being told to stop. The hoop is returned and the other players follow the same procedure. Any players knocking over the hoop while going through it has to go to the end of the line and try again. A team is penalized four points if the hoop is touched before it stops rolling. Any player throwing or rolling the hoop into foul territory may not run the bases.

HOOP BALL, *(cont'd.)*

TEACHING HINT: Remind the players that it is not important who goes through the hoop last, but how fast they go through.

VARIATIONS: Players can dribble a basketball or soccer ball while running the bases. An extra ball is used in this game. Player 1 for the team on the field, standing next to home, can start dribbling the ball toward the hoop after the player has thrown it. The player retrieving the hoop holds it while the first player passes the ball through the hoop to the rest of the team. Use the same scoring system.

A player rolls a tire, and the team on the field has to crawl through the tire being held by a teammate.

HOW FAST AM I?

OBJECTIVE: To score the most runs after two innings

EQUIPMENT: One 12″ softball and four gloves, bases, and cones for each game

SKILLS: Running, throwing, and catching

ORGANIZATION: Six teams with four on each team. Use a regular softball diamond or separate the bases by six feet. The team on the field has a player standing by each base. Place the ball on home plate and a cone three feet to the right of each base. Three games are played simultaneously.

HOW TO PLAY: The game starts when the catcher bends down to pick up the ball. The runner then leaves, staying to the right of all the cones. The fielder at each base has to catch the ball before throwing it to the next base. Any ball dropped has to be retrieved before the fielder can step on the base to throw the ball to the next base. Players continue throwing to each base until the catcher has the ball and is standing on home plate. The runner attempts to beat the throw to the catcher. If the runner is successful, the team receives one run. Each player has a turn before switching sides. After two rounds, the winning team on each field moves one field to the right and games start again. A runner who interferes with a fielder attempting to catch a ball by waving his or her arms or failing to run to the right of each cone is out.

HOW FAST AM I?, *(cont'd.)*

TEACHING HINTS: The runners must wear helmets when running the bases. Remind the players to use proper throwing technique and to keep hands relaxed when catching the ball.

VARIATIONS: Play the same way but use soccer skills. The fielding team has to pass the ball to each fielder, who has to control the ball before passing it to the next base. The runner has to dribble the ball around the cones.

Instead of having the winning team move to the next field, have all odd-numbered players rotate.

Have the catcher throw to first, first to third, third to second, and second to home. The runner circles the bases the same way.

MARATHON KICKBALL

OBJECTIVE: To score the most runs

EQUIPMENT: Three 8 1/2" playground balls and four bases

SKILLS: Kicking, running, throwing, and catching

ORGANIZATION: Two teams with twelve players on each team. Regular kickball or softball rules apply. The game is played on a softball diamond, with one team on the field playing all the positions. The kicking team has three or four minutes to score runs. Players kick in number order. All balls have to be quickly returned to the teacher or supervisor, who is the pitcher, when they are no longer involved in a play.

HOW TO PLAY: Any ball kicked may be used to get a runner or runners out. A warning is given to the fielding team if a player intentionally delays the return of a ball or balls to the pitcher. If it happens again, have all runners advance two bases and extend playing time another thirty seconds. A player makes an out by kicking two foul balls, having a fly ball caught, being forced at a base, or passing another runner—or when a thrown ball beats the runner going to a base and not being forced. When time has expired, give the score and have teams switch.

TEACHING HINT: Remind the players, for safety, to throw to a base the runner is running to—not at the runner.

VARIATIONS: Play the same game, using a tennis racquet and three tennis balls.

Use Footballs. The teacher throws the ball and the player has to catch it before punting it. If a player drops the throw, he or she may not run the bases and must wait for another turn. The same rules apply.

OPTION SOFTBALL

OBJECTIVE: To score the most runs

EQUIPMENT: Bats, a 12" rag ball, four bases, a catcher's mask, and softball gloves for every fielder

SKILLS: Hitting, throwing, catching, fielding ground balls, and running bases

ORGANIZATION: Two teams with twelve players on a team—one team playing the field. There are three outs per inning.

HOW TO PLAY: Regular softball rules apply with the following exceptions: Any player making an out while at bat is allowed to go to first base and run the bases, with the run counting if the runner scores. If a player receives ball four for a walk, he or she has the option of going to first base or, based on the number of strikes left, self-tossing the ball to hit it. If a player has two strikes left, he or she may self-toss the ball both times or do it once and, if not successful, take the walk. A batter is out if he or she does not hit the ball into fair territory on the last strike, if a fielder catches his or her fly ball, or if he or she is thrown out going to first base or passing another runner. Any batter throwing a bat does not get to run the bases.

TEACHING: Remind the player where all the possible plays are before each pitch. For safety, have the player stand by one foul line facing the hitter. If you have a backstop, have them stand behind it.

VARIATIONS: Play kickball the same way, with the kicker having the opportunity of going to first base after kicking three foul balls. A strike is made in this game when the ball goes directly over home plate and is not kicked. Use the same rules for strikes and balls. Player will kick a stationary ball or punt it. The pitcher has to wait until the kicker is ready before rolling the ball.

THREE UP—THREE OUTS

OBJECTIVE:	To score the most runs
EQUIPMENT:	Two 8 1/2″ playground balls and eight bases
SKILLS:	Kicking, catching, base running, and throwing
ORGANIZATION:	Eight teams with three players on each team. Four teams play on one diamond. Team 1 kicks first. Team 2 has a player pitching, one catching, and one playing first. Players on team 3 are at second, third, and shortstop. Team 4 plays the outfield. When teams rotate, each team plays the positions of the team in front of it in the order. Three outs per team are allowed. Any player making an out while going to first base will still be allowed to run the bases, but it counts as one team out.

THREE UP—THREE OUTS, *(cont'd.)*

HOW TO PLAY: To start the game, the pitcher rolls the ball to the first kicker, who attempts to get on base and score a run. The two teammates follow the same procedure. A player makes an out by kicking three foul balls, going past either foul line or home plate to kick a ball, having a fly ball caught, or being thrown out at first base. To retire a base runner, throw to the base the runner is approaching. If two players are on base, the lead runner has to score on a base hit. A runner does not have to score if there is a force-out or if a fly ball is caught.

TEACHING HINTS: Remind the players to throw to the base a runner is going to, not at the runner. Encourage base runners to be aggressive when they run the bases.

VARIATIONS: Use a 12″ or 16″ softball and play the same game.

Play "Work Up." When an out is made on a ground out or a force-out, the pitcher moves in to hit. A fly ball caught allows the player who caught it to go in and hit. When the pitcher goes in to bat, the fielder playing first base takes his or her place, and the player who threw the ball to first base, takes that player's place.

WALL BLAST

OBJECTIVE: To score the most points

EQUIPMENT: Sixteen cones and eight 7" playground balls

SKILLS: Throwing and catching

ORGANIZATION: The number of teams is determined by available wall space. There are three players per team, with each one having a number from one to three. Teams line up along one of the sidelines in file formation. A cone is placed ten feet in front of each team. Place the second cone either fifteen or twenty-five feet from the far wall. Age and ability will determine this distance. The first player in line has the ball. Teams stay to the right of their cones.

WALL BLAST, *(cont'd.)*

HOW TO PLAY: On a signal, the first player runs to the farthest cone and
throws the ball against the wall for the next player in line to
catch. The next in line leaves when the first player has passed
the closest cone, and this player attempts to catch the ball
before it hits the ground. If he or she is successful, this second
player immediately throws the ball against the wall for the
third player to catch. This procedure is followed by each team
for a set time limit, such as three minutes. Teams receive one
point for each successful catch. Players may not go past a cone
when throwing or catching a ball. If this happens on a thrown
ball, the player has to retrieve the ball and run around the
nearest cone directly in front of his or her team before throwing it again. If a player who is attempting to catch the ball goes
past the cone, the player has to retrieve the ball before throwing it against the wall. The player will not receive a point.

TEACHING HINT: Remind the players not to look at the ball after throwing it—to
eliminate any possibility of interfering with a teammate.

VARIATIONS: Half-court divides teams. Those on one half compete with one
another. The two winning teams on each half then challenge
each other.

  Tape a three-foot square on the wall ten feet from the floor.
Any ball landing inside this square is worth two points. A ball
touching a line is worth one point.

  Players can rotate one team on each successful catch. Time
how long it takes all players to return to their original teams.

VOLLEYBALL

ADD-IT-UP VOLLEYBALL

OBJECTIVE: To be the first team to reach twenty-one points

EQUIPMENT: One volleyball for each court

SKILLS: Serving, catching, bumping, setting, and spiking

ORGANIZATION: Four teams with six to eight on each team. Two teams on each court face each other on opposite sides of the net. Regular volleyball rules apply. A team is allowed one re-serve, which is taken ten feet closer to the net. One point is given for any serve or set going over the net, two points for a forearm pass (bump) kept in play and going over the net, and three points for any legal spike. Points are given to each team as the ball is being volleyed over the net.

ADD-IT-UP VOLLEYBALL, *(cont'd.)*

HOW TO PLAY: One team, determined by a coin flip, starts the game. A team receives points even when players hit the ball to teammates. Players in third and fourth grades have the option of catching the ball, hitting it directly over the net, or hitting it to a partner. Any player catching the ball does not receive points. Third graders may volley the ball any number of times before it has to go over the net. Fourth graders are limited to a maximum of five hits. Those in fifth and sixth grades follow the regular volleyball rules.

TEACHING HINT: Do not allow players to touch or go under the net.

VARIATIONS: See how many consecutive points can be scored by both teams before the ball touches the ground or goes out of play.

Place a long rope between the courts to divide them into four courts. Use two balls.

BUMP, SET, AND GO

OBJECTIVE: To be the first to completely switch sides, and then return

EQUIPMENT: Standards, plus one volleyball and net for each court

SKILLS: Serving, bumping, setting, and running

ORGANIZATION: Six teams with four players on each team. Two teams on each court face each other on opposite sides of the net. A coin flip determines which team serves first. All serves are taken from the right rear corner. Younger players may move ten feet closer. Players line up in regular volleyball positions.

HOW TO PLAY: The game is started with a serve. Once the ball has gone over the net, the receiving player immediately does a forearm (bump) back over the net. If the ball is successfully bumped back over the net, in bounds, these two players switch sides by running along the sidelines. If the ball is dropped by an opposing player, the one serving rotates one position with the next player serving. This format is continued until two teams have completely switched sides. The time it took them is the time to beat in the next game. Teams rotate one court to their right after each game. Opposing players may not interfere with one another when they are on the same side. Players who have already made the switch should set the ball to another player on the same side, so he or she can bump it over. Once a player changes sides, he or she has to remain there until everyone on his or her team is on the same side. Once this happens, players may start returning. Players may not switch if either player drops the ball.

BUMP, SET, AND GO, *(cont'd.)*

TEACHING HINTS: Remind the players to use proper technique when doing the forearm pass. Penalize any player who runs under the net by having that player return to where he or she started the game and begin again.

VARIATION: Play the same game, but use a beach ball.

METEORITE BALL

OBJECTIVE: For one team to have the fewest balls on their side of the net

EQUIPMENT: Seven balls for each court

SKILLS: Throwing and catching

ORGANIZATION: Four teams with six players on each team. Two teams face each other on opposite sides of the net. One team is give four balls and the other three balls. Two games are played at the same time.

HOW TO PLAY: On a signal, the balls are thrown over the net as rapidly as possible. Any ball that goes out of bounds, is dropped, hits the ground, or is either rolled or thrown under the net is taken out of the game and belongs to the team committing the infraction. Players may take only one step after catching the ball. After five minutes, or when all balls are out of the game, play stops. A team receives one point for each ball, and the team with the lowest total moves one court.

TEACHING HINT: Remind the players to throw to an open space, not directly at another player.

METEORITE BALL, *(cont'd.)*

VARIATIONS: Place a net between the two courts, going from one sideline to the other sideline. Have all four teams compete against one another. A team receives one point each time a ball lands on the team's court.

See how long all teams can keep the balls from touching the ground. Any ball touching the ground is taken out of the game. When the last ball touches the ground, the time is given and teams attempt to beat this time.

MOON BALL

OBJECTIVE: To see which team can keep the ball in play the longest

EQUIPMENT: Four rainbow balls or beach balls

SKILLS: Setting and bumping

ORGANIZATION: Four teams with six players on each team. The games are played on two volleyball courts—two teams on each court. Players number off from one to six. The first player on each team is holding the ball.

HOW TO PLAY: The first player on each court starts the game by hitting the ball into the air and calling, "One." The others, and in number order, attempt to keep the ball from touching the ground. Once a player hits the ball he or she may not hit it again until the next turn, in order. Any time a ball hits the ground, is touched by another player, or is caught, play stops and the score is given. This is the total to beat in the next game.

TEACHING HINT: Remind the players to get into the proper position to hit the ball.

VARIATION: The teams are in a shuttle formation. The object of the game is for the first player, on one side of the gym, to strike the ball (bump or set), and keep it in the air until he or she reaches the other side. The first player in line for the opposite team does the same thing. Continue this format until all players are back where they started. If the ball touches the ground, the teams receive that score and go again. Do not use a net for this game.

POP THE BALL

OBJECTIVE:	To see how long teams can volley a ball
EQUIPMENT:	Four volleyballs
SKILLS:	Bumping and setting
ORGANIZATION:	Four teams with six players on each team. The game is played on a basketball court or field. Each team forms a large circle on one quarter of the court. One player on each team is holding the volleyball.
HOW TO PLAY:	On a signal, the player holding the ball starts the game by throwing it up, then either bumps or sets it to another player. Any player failing to bump or set the ball to another player must immediately put the ball back into play. A player may not return a ball to the player hitting it to her or him, or catch the ball before volleying it to another player. The teams are timed to see how long the ball can be successfully volleyed. They also receive one point for each successful volley.
TEACHING HINT:	Remind the players to form a triangle with their thumbs and index fingers when setting.
VARIATIONS:	Use only the forearm pass (bump) to play this game. Have the players line up in a straight line facing a wall, instead of in a circle. In this game, each player takes his or her turn volleying the ball over a 7' mark on the wall. The object is to see how many consecutive volleys each team can make.

RAINBOW VOLLEYBALL

OBJECTIVE: To be the first team to reach twenty-one points

EQUIPMENT: One beach ball or rainbow ball for each court

SKILLS: Serving, setting, bumping, digging, and spiking

ORGANIZATION: Four teams with six to eight players on each team. Two teams face each other on opposite sides of the net; two games are played at the same time. Teams number off from one to four, with odd-numbered teams serving first.

HOW TO PLAY: Any serve crossing the net, or hitting the ceiling, standards, lights, backboards, or back wall is considered a good serve. Any serve landing out of bounds, either by half-court or the end line, means a side out. Players receiving the serve may hit the ball either on the first bounce or directly over the net. Players may not catch the ball or use open palms below the waist to volley the ball. Players rotate after every serve, whether scoring or on loss of serve. The ball may be volleyed any number of times by one player or several.

RAINBOW VOLLEYBALL, *(cont'd.)*

TEACHING HINTS: Remind the players, for safety, not to touch the net or to use a fist when hitting the ball. Encourage the players to set one another up for an attack.

VARIATIONS: Players are limited to one hit, unless the ball has been hit by another player. Time to see how long two teams can keep the ball in play.

All Gym Volleyball. Use the same rules as above, except the serve is taken from one sideline by half-court. The serve may be hit anywhere on the opponents' side of the net. Back line players rotate to the left, with the front line players moving to the right.

Play the same game, but use two balls. Both serves are taken at the same time and play continues until both balls are out of play. Teams receive one point for each ball landing on their side.

SLOW-MOTION VOLLEYBALL

OBJECTIVE: To be the first team to reach fifteen points

EQUIPMENT: One plastic golfing tube for each player and one balloon for each court.

SKILL: Striking

ORGANIZATION: Four teams with six on each team. Two teams face each other on opposite courts; two games are played at the same time. All serves are from the right rear corner of the court. Each player is holding a tube and the one serving is also holding the balloon. The team going first is determined by a coin flip. The net is six feet high, with court dimensions determined by available space.

SLOW-MOTION VOLLEYBALL, *(cont'd.)*

HOW TO PLAY: The first player starts the game by hitting the balloon with his or her tube. Once the balloon has been put in play, players continue hitting it until it goes over the net. Front line players may hit it either over the net or to another front line player. Players continue volleying the balloon until one team makes a mistake. If a balloon touches the floor, or a player goes under the net or touches it, the team loses serve or a point. A player has only one serve each time, whether he or she scores a point or not. Any balloon going past the sideline may be kept in play as long as it does not enter the other court. Back line players may not volley the balloon over the net and must remain behind the front line players. Once the serve is finished, players may hit the balloon any number of times to get it to a front line player over the net.

TEACHING HINT: Remind the players to call out, "Mine," when they go for the balloon, and to remain within their own area.

VARIATIONS: Allow only one consecutive hit for a player each time.
    Use two balloons with serves being taken at the same time.

WALL BALL

OBJECTIVE: To be the team with the lowest point total after serving and setting a ball against the wall

EQUIPMENT: Five volleyballs

SKILLS: Serving, setting, and catching

ORGANIZATION: Five teams with five players on each team. One player from each team forms a group, with one player from each team at the head of one group. The first player has a ball. A serving line is ten feet from the wall. After four minutes, all odd-numbered players rotate one team to the left and even-numbered players to the right.

```
              7'  MARK

              W A L L

       SERVING      LINE
    1      2      3      4      5
    2      3      4      5      1
    3      4      5      1      2
    4      5      1      2      3
    5      1      2      3      4
```

HOW TO PLAY: The game starts with the first player serving the ball over the 7' mark on the wall. After serving the ball, the player goes to the end of the line. The next in line, when the serve is good, catches the ball and sets it above the same mark before going to the end of the line. Players continue this rotation until someone commits an infraction. Players in fifth grade and up may not catch the ball. A player who does receives one point and starts the next game with a serve. Players receive points for double-hitting a ball, interfering with another player, not keeping the ball in the designated area, hitting the wall below the mark, or failing to catch the ball. When the game is over, total the score and switch.

TEACHING HINTS: Keep groups far enough apart to reduce the chance of a collision. Encourage players to use good technique when setting and serving the ball.

WALL BALL, *(cont'd.)*

VARIATIONS: Have the players line up by teams. Play the game the same way. The lowest point total is the total to beat.

Start the game the same way, but after each successful hit have the player rotate one team to his or her right. Continue until all players return to their own teams and in the original order. This is timed, and when all teams are finished, they attempt to beat their time. Players returning to their own teams go to the end of the line.